A Celebration of

Praise

A Celebration of

Praise

Stand Amazed at Who God Is!

DICK EASTMAN

Chosen Books

A Division of Baker Book House Co
Grand Rapids, Michigan 49516

Published by Chosen Books
a division of Baker Book House Company
P.O. Box 6287, Grand Rapids, MI 49516-6287
www.bakerbooks.com

Previously published by Baker Books

Printed in the United States of America

Library of Congress Cataloging-in-Publication Data
Eastman, Dick.
    A celebration of praise : stand amazed at who God is! / Dick Eastman.
        p.   cm.
    Includes bibliographical references.
    ISBN 0-8007-9327-7 (pbk.)
    1. God—Meditations. 2. Praise of God—Meditations. I. Title.
BT103 .E27 2003
242′.72—dc21   2002014612

Unless otherwise indicated, all Scripture quotations are taken from the *Holy Bible, New Living Translation*, copyright © 1996. Used by permission of Tyndale House Publishers, Inc., Wheaton, IL 60189. All rights reserved.

Scripture marked kjv is taken from the King James Version of the Bible.

Scripture marked nkjv is taken from the New King James Version. Copyright © 1979, 1980, 1982 by Thomas Nelson, Inc. Used by permission. All rights reserved.

Scripture marked niv is taken from the HOLY BIBLE, NEW INTERNATIONAL VERSION®. NIV®. Copyright © 1973, 1978, 1984 by International Bible Society. Used by permission of Zondervan. All rights reserved.

Scripture marked tlb is taken from *The Living Bible* © 1971. Used by permission of Tyndale House Publishers, Inc., Wheaton, IL 60189. All rights reserved.

The definitions of praise words that appear in part 2 are the author's compilations from various standard research sources based on a pneumatological study of each word as it would apply to the Supreme Being, God Almighty.

For information concerning prayer helps mentioned in this book, the reader may contact:

Every Home for Christ
P.O. Box 64000
Colorado Springs, CO 80962

To
The Composers of Sacred Song,
May your music magnify the majesty of God!

Contents

In the house of God there is never-ending festival; the angel choir makes eternal holiday; the presence of God's face gives joy that never fails. And from that everlasting, perpetual festivity there sounds in the ears of the heart a strain, mysterious, melodious, sweet—provided the world does not drown it.

St. Augustine
from *Patrologia Latina*

A Cause for Celebration

They will celebrate your abundant goodness and joyfully sing of your righteousness.

Psalm 145:7 NIV

It was a startling thought. And I knew instantly that God planted it in my heart. It happened in our "Office of Worship and Intercession," a special place of prayer established at the start of our ministry where prayer continued on a regular basis throughout office hours. We prayed primarily for other intercessors—those who, because of their commitments in prayer, were under unusually heavy spiritual attack. We were determined to engage in spiritual warfare for others engaged in such warfare. The room served as a constant reminder that prayer and worship were as vital to our ministry as any other activity. Today, this same commitment is expanding significantly as Every Home for Christ establishes the Jericho Center, its international ministry center in Colorado Springs where worship and intercession will continue day and night.

In this setting God impressed on my heart the far-reaching power of worship-saturated intercession. As usual, our entire staff had gathered at the beginning of the day for prayer. On this particular occasion we would be together for almost an hour. Our volunteer intercessors, or staff-intercessors, would continue in prayer for the rest of the day.

That day a lesson would be learned that would touch the whole of our ministry and would ultimately result in this book. It was a lesson that continues to be foundational to the ministry of Every Home for Christ to this day, now conducting home-to-home evangelism campaigns in more than one hundred nations. It was also a lesson that demonstrated how little we understood about the fullness of praise. A staff member, thumbing through several of the numerous requests received by our ministry from other intercessors and supporters, began to weep as she read of the many difficult needs shared by those "under attack" because of prayer commitments.

"These people are desperate," she said with tears, "and they're counting on us to stand with them in prayer." Pausing for a moment, she added, "And there's so many of them—I just don't know how we can give them the prayer attention they deserve."

By now, the staff worker was sobbing; I, too, began to weep, but my tears turned to a river of joy as an inward impression from the Lord saturated my thoughts: *"You will triumph in My praise."*

I did not hear an audible voice, but I knew God was communicating something vital within my spirit. After pondering the thought, I quietly prayed, "Lord, what does this mean?"

His response revealed a reality I had contemplated for years but had never completely understood or applied: *All of our victories, whether they result in an instantaneous deliverance from a circumstance or are simply the strength to endure a long and difficult trial, flow from God's nature and character alone. God's presence is our victory and praise makes room for the fullness of His presence.*

It was a powerful thought and as our worship continued that morning, I was reminded of a biblical basis on which I could accept these inward impressions as truly from the Lord. The psalmist wrote that God "inhabitest the praises of Israel [or His people]" (Ps. 22:3 KJV). And this means, as the Hebrew text bears out, that God's very throne is established where His people praise Him. He literally dwells amid the praises of His children. Or, as the New American Standard version of the Bible emphasizes in a footnote for Psalm 22:3, "Thou who art enthroned upon the praises of Israel." Further, where God's presence dwells, His power must function in its absolute fullness. And since Satan cannot operate in God's presence, to saturate our prayers with the high praises of God is to saturate the circumstances represented by those prayers with the very presence of God. We could, indeed, "glory" or "triumph" in God's praise.

Some weeks later I joyfully discovered the uniqueness of a prayer uttered by the psalmist. He asked the Lord to let Israel honor the Lord's name and "triumph" (or *glory*) in His praise (Ps. 106:47 KJV).

The Hebrew word translated "triumph" in the Authorized Version of Psalm 106:47 is generally translated "glory" by Hebrew scholars and suggests an almost ecstatic shout of victory over a defeated foe. It seems to suggest the idea of exaltation to a position of victory over an enemy in order to celebrate with a shout of triumph. In a sense, the psalmist was asking God to grant a victory over Israel's enemies so they might enjoy a celebration of praise.

As our prayers continued that morning I felt God was saying more. There was the clear sense that our praises were not merely something we would do *after* a victory but that these praises actually would contribute to future victories. Effective praise truly would lead to a glorious cause for celebration. Our praises, like those of Paul and Silas in Acts 16:25, somehow would be involved in releasing these victories. A similar thought is suggested by the psalmist but is amplified to touch the whole world. Psalm 67:5–7 states, "May the nations praise you, O God. . . .

Then the earth will yield its harvests, . . . and people all over the world will fear him."

It became evident that if God indeed was leading us to greater heights in victorious praise, we had to learn about the true nature of praise and how to sustain it. Further, we had to learn that our praises should not be offered simply because they seem to bring nice results but because God is worthy of them. In other words, although favorable results would be forthcoming, all of our praise must have God, alone, as the foundational focus. Simply stated, the essence of all praise is to stand amazed at who God is!

Understanding Praise

From the moment our prayers ended that day, our staff made a commitment to pursue a richer and deeper understanding of the manner and method of offering sustained, biblical praise.

But what does it truly mean to sustain our praises? Years ago I learned that praise is the act of verbalized worship or adoration that declares or acknowledges God for *who* He is. Thanksgiving, on the other hand, is the act of offering specific thanks to God for things He has done for us or others.

I knew that praise is recognizing God's nature or character with my words. However, I lacked sufficient knowledge of God's character and nature to help make my times of praise truly meaningful.

Sadly, many of my praise experiences sounded something like this—"God, I praise You because You are wonderful . . . beautiful . . . magnificent . . . and a lot of other nice things, I'm sure." The fact is, I did not have the slightest idea what other praise expressions might come under the category of nice things that could be said of God.

That had to change, I decided, so a few days later I grabbed *Webster's Instant Word Guide* with its thirty-five thousand entries and searched for every word that expressed "good" or "right." My thought was that any word in our language that pictures anything that is "sound," like purity or goodness, must have its roots in God, for God alone is eternally good and sound, and all that He does is absolutely right. My research uncovered almost five hundred distinct ways that I might praise the Lord. I greatly reduced this number when compiling this book in order to provide a practical approach to developing systematic, sustained praise.

As I began to search the Bible for verses to support these various praise words, I was delighted to find hundreds of examples of specific, biblical ways to apply these words in praise. It quickly became apparent that I needed a systematic plan to learn them as well as to teach them to others.

At the suggestion of a friend, I decided to develop a seven-week plan. It would be a "praise strategy" that would focus on seven different ways to praise the Lord each week with several related scriptural references for each aspect of praise. Naturally, all of these concepts of praise might be employed at any time but having a systematic plan makes it easier to learn them, and possibly memorize them, for greater spontaneity of praise in the future. Although this list is complete in relation to main praise themes, it also is vastly incomplete when the full possibilities of praise are considered.

It likewise is important to remember that all true praise essentially must focus on the nature and character of God. For this reason I have chosen to divide this book into two distinct parts. Part 1 examines a variety of general aspects related to God's character and nature. It is included to provide an overview of our wonderful God who is truly deserving of praise. Part 2, the real purpose of this book, presents a systematic guide for praising God each day. Because part 1 includes a somewhat theological overview of God, I have chosen to rely heavily on the insights of several noted theologians and authors. I am deeply indebted for their contributions and for the permission from their publishers to quote extensively from their writings. Please do not become burdened by any of what might be termed the "heavy" portions of part 1. They are included to help you stop and contemplate the true depth of God's infinite nature.

Practical Suggestions

Because the most important result of studying the following pages is to develop a meaningful praise experience as a part of your devotional habit, I suggest you consider purchasing inexpensive plastic tabs at a stationery store for the purpose of separating the various weekly sections in part 2. Self-adhesive tabs can be attached to the page featuring the first praise word of each weekly section. This system will help you find any specific praise list quickly during your devotional hour. Use a felt-tip color highlighter to shade specific portions of Bible verses that directly relate to a particular praise word.

The many praise themes from part 2 may be easily adapted for use in corporate prayer gatherings as a stimulus for bringing more substantive praise into such meetings.

There is an introductory meditation on the Sunday word for each week that explores in depth one of God's characteristics: love, holiness, majesty, justice, faithfulness, mercy, integrity. The meditations demonstrate the potential use of each praise word. Notice that the praise words for the week are not grouped under a single theme but rather reflect the limitless qualities of our Father God. The day will come when you'll have many, if not all, of these praise words (and some of their scriptural references) committed to memory. And best of all, every devotional hour will become a *cause for celebration.*

Part 1

The Object of Our Praise

The gifted writer S. D. Gordon tells of an elderly Christian whose advancing years had taken their toll on her memory. As her health faded the time came when she could recite but a single verse—2 Timothy 1:12: ". . . I know whom I have believed, and am persuaded that he is able to keep that which I have committed unto him against that day" (RSV). Even these words slowly slipped from her memory until only a few days of her life remained and friends would hear her repeat just seven words: "That which I have committed unto Him."

Finally, as the hour of the woman's death neared and her memory was all but gone, she voiced a single word repeatedly. It was all she could remember—"Him, Him, Him!"

Said Gordon, "She had lost the whole Bible, except for that one powerful word. But yet she *had* the whole Bible in that one word—Him!"

Here, beloved, is the key to any meaningful study of praise. Effective praise has its focus on our Lord alone. The more we are able to focus our praises exclusively on the nature and character of God the Father, the Son, and the Holy Spirit, the more power we will experience as the result of that praise.

Sadly, so many Christians these days are consumed with a concern for material things. They sometimes inadvertently misuse the word *praise* by relating it to thanksgiving. How often do we say in prayer, "I praise You, God, for my new house," or, "I praise You, Lord, for giving me an increase in my salary." These statements are expressions of thanksgiving rather than declarations of true praise. Although thanksgiving is a powerful part of our maturing process in total worship, the sad reality is that many of us lose sight of the true focus of praise—God Himself.

A. W. Tozer advises, "It is not a cheerful thought that millions of us who live in a land of Bibles, who belong to churches and labor to promote the Christian religion, may yet pass our whole life on this earth without once having thought or tried to think seriously about the being of God."[1]

Truly a greater understanding of the God of all creation must be realized if we are to maximize our praise. And only by a careful searching out of God's nature can He be fully understood. Nineteenth-century theologian William B. Pope expressed, "Every thought of God involves the thought of His attributes: without these He is verily and indeed an unknown and unknowable God."[2]

It is quite impossible, then, to fully know God until we have some foundational understanding of who God is and what He is like. Pope further asserts, "The meditation and study of God's Divine attributes lies at the foundation of all theology, which is by that very term the doctrine of God contemplated in Himself and in His universal relations, or in the universal relation of all things to Him."[3]

In the same way that meditation and the study of God's attributes lies at the foundation of theology, the praise and adoration of God's attributes lies at the foundation of all spiritual power. This thought is substantiated by Psalm 22:3. Because God inhabits the praises of His people, that verse tells us, He literally sets up His throne, or "dwells" where His people praise Him. In other words, all of God's power is present where there is true worship. We will, indeed, *triumph in His praise.*

Thus, to focus praise completely on God, including a verbalized recognition of His nature and character, leads to an unbounded release of God's power. It likewise leads to special growth in such vital qualities of maturity as humility and meekness. Julian of Norwich wrote, "For of all things the beholding and the loving of the Maker maketh the soul to seem less in his own sight, and most filleth him with reverent dread and true meekness; and with plenty of charity for his fellow Christians."[4]

God's Reality

Herman Bavinck, in a substantive analysis of God's attributes, suggests that the very fact we are able to name the attributes of God proves that they were revealed by God. Bavinck explains, "We need the idea of time in order to obtain a conception of God's eternity, and that of space in order to form an idea of His omnipresence, and that of the finite in order for us to become aware of His infinitude and immutability."[5]

Recognizing the reality of God is the first vital step leading to a life of true purpose-filled praise. James I. Packer focuses special attention on our need to understand the character of God in his well-prepared study, *Knowing God*. Because of the value of Packer's insights to Part 1 of our study, it is appropriate at this point to rely heavily on his thoughts.

On the importance of the study of God, Packer writes, "Disregard the study of God, and you sentence yourself to stumble and blunder through life blindfolded, as it were, with no sense of direction and no understanding of what surrounds you."[6] He elaborates,

What is my ultimate aim and object in occupying my mind with these things? What do I intend to do with my knowledge about God, once I have got it? For the fact that we have to face is this: that if we pursue theological knowledge for its own sake, it is bound to go bad on us. It will make us proud and conceited. The very greatness of the subject matter will intoxicate us, and we shall come to think of ourselves as a cut above other Christians because of our interest in it and grasp of it.[7]

We must seek, in studying God, to be led to God. It was for this purpose that revelation was given, and it is to this use that we must put it.[8]

How can we turn our knowledge *about* God into knowledge *of* God? The rule for doing this is demanding, but simple. It is that we turn each truth that we learn *about* God into matter for meditation *before* God, leading to prayer and praise *to* God.[9]

Knowing God, then, is vital for effective praise. But mark it clearly; knowing God is not an experience of the intellect but an encounter of the heart. Packer stresses, "Interest in theology, and knowledge about God, and the capacity to think clearly and talk well on Christian themes, is not at all the same thing as knowing Him. We may know as much about God as Calvin knew—indeed, if we study his works diligently, sooner or later we shall—and yet all the time (unlike Calvin may I say) we may hardly know God at all."[10]

God, indeed, wants us to know Him, and not merely casually but intimately. Simply stated, God's design is to reveal Himself to man. In the first declaration about Himself, "I am God Almighty; serve me faithfully and live a blameless life" (Gen. 17:1), and throughout the Bible, the God whose character is the standard of perfection, whose unbounded all-sufficiency is the source of strength and whose presence is the manifestation of absolute light and love itself, is revealed. Repeatedly in Scripture a presentation of His names, or, a presentation of revelation insights that combine His essence and His attributes, are found.

He continually reveals who He is. "I am Jehovah," He tells us, the absolute self-sufficient Being. He is *Spirit*, we further discover, which reveals Him to be the personal object of our worship. He is *Light,* which pictures His purity in contrast to mankind's impurities. Finally, He declares that He is *Love,* the total of all that is caring and giving.

The truly exciting thing about recognizing this, specifically within the context of praising God for all that He is, is the purpose and meaning it adds to our Christian experience. Packer suggests, "What makes life worthwhile is having a big enough objective, something which catches our imagination and lays hold of our intelligence; and this the Christian has, in a way that no other man has. For what higher, more exalted, and more compelling goal can there be than to know God?"[11] He elaborates, "What were we made for? To know God. What aim should we set ourselves in life? To know God. What is 'the eternal life' that Jesus gives? Knowledge of God. 'This is life eternal, that they might know thee the only true God, and Jesus Christ, whom thou hast sent' (John 17:3)."[12] To this might be added the powerful prayer testimony of Paul, "I keep asking that the God of our Lord Jesus Christ, the glorious Father, may give you the Spirit of wisdom and revelation, so that you may know him better" (Eph. 1:17 NIV).

And what can we expect this increased knowledge of God to produce in us? Packer offers this response: "Men who know their God are before anything else men who pray, and the first point where their zeal and energy for God's glory come to expression is in their prayers. . . . The invariable fruit of true knowledge of God is energy to pray for God's cause—energy, indeed, which can only find an outlet and a relief of inner tension when channeled into such prayer—and the more knowledge, the more energy!"[13]

Our capacity to praise God effectively, then, is directly related to our grasp of God's nature and character. Packer suggests that *energy* for prayer is found in an increased knowledge of God. Perhaps all meaningful *substance* for praise is found in a similar knowledge. Thus, the more substantive I wish my praise to be, the more mindful I must become of *all* God is. As an unknown poet wisely penned:

'Tis what I know of Thee,
My Lord, my God,
That fills my heart with praise,
My lips with song!

God's Unity

To further explore the nature and character of God, it is not only important but vital to understand the unity that exists between *all* His characteristics. Theologian Herman Bavinck explains why we even attempt to define different attributes of God when God is clearly a single Divine entity. He states,

> Although every attribute we might suggest is identical with God's being, nevertheless, distinctions must be made: the attributes do not differ in substance; nor, on the other hand, is the difference a merely verbal one; they differ in "thought" i.e., each attribute expresses a distinct something. . . . Though in God holiness and righteousness are identical, nevertheless, we distinguish them in thought.[14]
>
> Every one of God's attributes is identical with His being: God's attributes do not differ from His essence nor from one another. . . . When the Christian theologian speaks of God's essence he is not speaking of one fundamental attribute from which the others are derived, but he refers to an essence which is identical with supreme life, supreme wisdom, supreme love, etc.[15]

William B. Pope adds succinctly, "The attributes of God are one in God, yet many to us."[16]

God's Totality

In evaluating a simplified overview of God's essence, not only must we recognize the unity of His attributes but that which seems almost synonymous—their totality. Bavinck states, "God is the real, the true essence, the fullness of essence, the sum total of all reality and perfection, the totality of essence, to which all other essence owes its origin, an ocean of essence, unbounded and immeasurable, the absolute Being, the only Being who has the ground of His existence in Himself."[17]

Because of God's unbounded essence, Bavinck points out, God's essence is, of necessity, infinitely rich, and therefore cannot be seen at a glance. In the same sense that a child is incapable of conceiving the value of a coin of a higher denomination until its worth is counted out to him by means of a number of coins of lesser denomination, similarly we are unable to conceive of the infinite fullness of God's essence unless it is revealed to us one step at a time, from a variety of angles and perspectives.

Bavinck sums it up well by suggesting that "God remains eternally and immutably the same, but He assumes different relations to His creatures and they enter into various relations with respect to Him. Light remains the same in essence even though in the spectrum it is broken up into various individual colors. . . . Fire does not change whether it warms, illumines, or burns. In addressing God we use various names because of the 'various effects' of His unchanging essence upon creatures. In this connection we must not forget the close relationship which is between God and His creatures."[18]

In attempting to comprehend God's unity and totality, it must be understood that every attribute that might be assigned to God's essence is identical with His being. In other words, Bavinck suggests, God is what He is. When God's essence is discussed, it must be remembered that each of His attributes is identical with who He is. Bavinck explains, "Whatever God is, He is completely and simultaneously."[19]

Thus, to praise God for any of the items on our daily list is to praise Him for all of those aspects of His nature. All are interrelated because God is all of each attribute—all of the time. God is, for example, holy in His justice and just in His holiness. He is faithful in His kindness and kind in His faithfulness.

God's Complexity

Praise also becomes exciting when God's unusual complexity is recognized. We can never "out praise" God! William B. Pope explains, "There is a sense indeed in which the being of God is absolutely undefinable, because He is absolutely incomprehensible."[20] Packer adds, "It is clear, to start with, that 'knowing' God is of necessity a more complex business than 'knowing' a fellow-man just as 'knowing' my neighbor is a more complex business than 'knowing' a house, or a book, or a language. The more complex the object, the more complex is the knowing of it. Knowledge of something abstract, like a language, is acquired by learning; knowledge of something inanimate, like . . . the British Museum, comes by inspection and exploration."[21]

Naturally, anyone attempting a study that even suggests the thought of "complete praise" must sooner or later face the question—how many divine attributes are there? A. W. Tozer responds, "Religious thinkers have differed about this. Some have insisted that there are seven, (including spirituality, infinity, eternity, immensity, necessary self-sufficiency, unchangeableness, and perfection), but Frederick Faber sang of the 'God of a thousand attributes' and Charles Wesley exclaimed,

Sovereign Father, heavenly king,
Thee we now presume to sing;
Glad Thine attributes confess,
Glorious all, and numberless."[22]

As suggested in the discussion of God's totality, God is one essence and yet might be described in many ways. This fact further reveals the complexity of His being, which, rather than stifling our capacity to praise Him, greatly enhances it. Bavinck states,

There is not a single name which adequately expresses God's being, but there are many names, properties, ideas, dignities by means of which some characteristic of God is revealed to us. . . . In God to *be* is the same as *to be strong* or *to be wise,* etc. That which is justice is also itself goodness, and that which is goodness is also itself blessedness. His greatness is the same as His wisdom, for He is not greater in size than is His virtue; and His goodness is the same as His wisdom and His greatness; and His truth is the same as all of these; and with respect to Him it is not one thing to be blessed and another thing to be great or wise or true or to be good, or, in general, to be Himself.[23]

The complexity of God, then, is something that must be accepted if we are to grasp even a basic recognition of the infinite possibilities of praise. At times, our minds may be taxed to their limits.

God's Simplicity

Only God at the same time can be complex *and* simple. Pope emphasizes that no being or essence is conceivable apart from its attributes and qualities.[24] Thus, God's very intention in revealing to us His nature and character declares His desire that we further explore His character and nature. Here we discover God's simplicity. He has revealed to us His character so that we might understand it better. It is His way of increasing our capacity to know Him.

It seems paradoxical to say that the attributes of God reveal both His complexity and simplicity. Even the church fathers regarded God as both unknowable and knowable. They described Him as unknowable in His essence but knowable in His revelation.

Bavinck provides further insight into God's simplicity: "Just because everything is *from* God, everything points back *to* God. Whoever wishes to think or speak about God must needs operate with forms and images borrowed from the world round about him."[25] God, indeed, reveals Himself to us in a multitude of simple ways from everyday life.

Providing further fuel for our understanding of God's simplicity, Tozer relates, "An attribute as we can know it, is a mental concept, an answer to a question, the reply which God makes to our interrogation concerning Himself."[26]

Simply stated, when man cries out to know God, God answers back by providing a revelation of His attributes.

It is imperative to recognize that God's intention in revealing His nature and character to us is to understand Him better. Pope states, "By referring to God's divine attributes we are referring to the full assemblage of those perfections which God ascribes to Himself in His Word: partly as the fuller explanation of His name, and partly as a design to regulate our conception of His character."[27]

God's Infinity

That quality of God's essence referred to as His infinity also is essential to our overview of God's nature. Spinoza suggests that God is "the soul, infinite, and necessarily existing substance, the absolute infinite Being, the absolutely first and immanent cause."[28] He further asserts, "The number of attributes pertaining to any object varies directly with its degree of reality; hence, God, as *infinite* reality must be *infinite* in the number of His attributes. . . ."[29]

Bavinck adds, "According to Reinhard, it is very probable that God might possess 'a great multitude of attributes (properties) of which we have not conception, seeing that it is altogether impossible for infinite perfection to unite with Himself all resemblances with the narrow confines of our creaturely existence.'"[30]

The reality of God's infinity is difficult to comprehend but is vital to an overall understanding of God. Pope stresses, "There is no idea concerning God more necessary to the human mind than that He is infinite in His being and perfections and all that is His: that whatever is to be predicated of His is to be infinitely predicated, or without limitation."[31]

God's character and attributes, then, must be described as infinitely limitless.

His holiness, for example, is limitless and therefore words to describe His holiness must be limitless. Likewise, His love, mercy, truth or any other attribute must be limitless. God is all that He is, and He is all of these things infinitely. Glory to God!

God's Eternity and Immensity

࿇

There is more that can be said about God, in a general sense, to help us prepare our understanding for praise. God is both eternal *and* immense. He exists for all eternity, while at the same time His presence fills the entire universe of known and unknown space.

Pope explains, "The immensity of God is only once declared in Scripture, but when it is said that 'Behold, the heaven and heaven of heavens cannot contain thee' (1 Kings 8:27), a formula is used which precisely defines the supremacy of the Eternal Spirit over all conditions of space."[32]

Pope further discusses God's eternity in relation to His immensity. He writes, "What the Divine immensity is to space the Divine eternity is to time. That God is eternal is the constant declaration of Scripture: in fact, this is a predicate more habitual than any other, being the first revelation of Himself to His people, I AM THAT I AM (Exod. 3:14), and continued in a variety of other forms down to the end, when Scripture refers to the God 'which is, and which was, and which is to come, the Almighty' (Rev. 1:8)."

Pope concludes, "And this is the deep perplexity of our human intellect, which however must accept the profound meaning of the name I AM, as teaching an eternal now enfolding and surrounding the successive existence of time . . . without distinction of past and present and future: that is, of past or present and future as measured in time and regulated by motion in space."[33]

God's Self-Sufficiency

Because every living organism depends on circumstances or situations outside of itself that affect its existence, it is virtually impossible to conceive of anything functioning independently. Yet, this is the case with God. Pope writes, "No notion we can form of God is more important in its meaning than that He is self-sufficient. All things have their cause and their end in Him. He is the one, whole, self-originated, independent, unconditioned and absolute Being. Here again the eternal name Jehovah, I AM, comes in."[34] He adds, "God simply, purely, and eternally *IS!* He is a being who needs nothing to complement or complete His perfection. . . . His self-sufficiency knows no limit but what He Himself by word or act assigns to it."[35]

And what does this mean to the Christian in pursuit of perfecting praise for the glory of God? It is a continual reminder that God in all His sufficiency becomes our sufficiency. *We* can be holy because *He* is holy and we draw our holiness from Him. All that He is He will always be. Our supply of His resources is inexhaustible.

God's Immutability

Equally exciting to the praise warrior is the immutability of God. God will never change. Pope states, "This attribute excludes all necessity of becoming, or development, and whatever is meant by change, or the possibility of change. In His essence and in all the attributes of His essential Being, God is forever the same."[36]

Think of it! God is infinitely and absolutely unchangeable. His glory will always be His glory and His power will always be His power. His essence is infinite; it has no beginning or ending. All that comprises His essence also is infinite. This also is true of His immutability. God is *infinitely* immutable. Thus, any quality of God's character or nature that we might possibly conceive of as being a focal point for praise will *always* be a focal point for praise. So utilizing the praise list in part 2 of this book is, in actuality, *practice for eternity!*

God's Incarnation

It would be a point of neglect if we failed to mention God's revelation of His nature *within* the context of human experience, in that event we call His incarnation. I refer, of course, to God becoming a man in Jesus Christ. Pope writes, "Every Christian theologian should remember that all Divine perfections must be contemplated as they are manifested and made incarnate in our Lord and Savior Jesus Christ. He is the sum of all Divine attributes in human nature."[37]

Emphasizing the supreme importance this factor holds for believers, Pope concludes, "In our perfection in Christ we shall be restored to the most consummate reflection of every attribute of the Creator which is impossible to finite man."[38]

Christ, indeed, is a direct reflection of God's very essence. He is the *Word*. Jesus Christ was and is God's expression of Himself to man. And just as we use words to express ourselves to others, God communicated who He is by sending Jesus Christ (His Word) to dwell among us. "The Son is the radiance of God's glory and the exact representation of his being" (Heb. 1:3 NIV).

Taste and See

~~~
❧
~~~

But what does all this mean for us? These attributes of God can be discussed and studied in an in-depth manner. However, until they are contemplated for the purpose of employing them in practical praise, they will have little, if any, effect on truly helping us grow in God.

With this in mind, it is time to begin the practical part of our study. We approached this subject with the expressed desire of perfecting our praise in God—as far as such a goal is possible. Packer suggests, "We are in the position of travelers who, after surveying a great mountain from afar, traveling around it and observing how it dominates the landscape and determines the features of the surrounding countryside, now approach it directly, for the intention of climbing it."[39]

The moment has arrived, beloved, to climb this mountain of praise before us. It is time to respond in anticipation to the psalmist's plea, "Taste and see that the Lord is good . . ." (Ps. 34:8).

To challenge us as we begin our journey, we look to the inspiring words of Charles H. Spurgeon, who, at twenty years of age, stood in the pulpit of the New Park Street Chapel in Southwark, England, and preached: "The highest science, the loftiest speculation, the mightiest philosophy, which can ever engage the attention of a child of God, is the name, the nature, the person, the work, the doings, and the existence of the great God whom he calls his Father."

Spurgeon's Sunday morning sermon was a call to a new awareness of the God who loves us infinitely and sent His Son to redeem us eternally. With an intensity that would mark his ministry for many years to come, he continued:

There is something exceedingly *improving to the mind* in a contemplation of the Divinity. It is a subject so vast, that our thoughts are lost in its immensity; so deep that our pride is drowned in its infinity. . . . No subject of contemplation will tend more to humble the mind, than thoughts of God. . . .

But while the subject *humbles* the mind, it also *expands* it. . . . Nothing will so enlarge the intellect, nothing so magnify the whole soul of man, as a devout, earnest, continued investigation of the great subject of the Deity. . . . So, go, plunge yourself in the Godhead's deepest sea: be lost in its immensity; and you shall come forth as from a couch of rest, refreshed and invigorated. I know nothing which can so comfort the soul; so calm the swelling billows of sorrow and grief; so speak peace to the winds of trial, as a devout musing upon the subject of the Godhead.[40]

God's Character Amplified

Finally, a study of God's character for the purpose of developing praise is not to be viewed as a monastic-like retreat from worldwide concerns, it is actually a major step toward direct involvement in what ultimately creates the proper climate for a worldwide spiritual awakening. In defining true revival, Bible teacher Joy Dawson states, "Revival is an amplification of God's character to His children—especially an amplification of His holiness."

Thus, any spiritual participation that turns our attention toward the worship of God's nature and character (such as His holiness) actually helps bring about the conditions that are foundational to a true spiritual awakening.

Dawson further explains, "Satan's chief desire is that God's children will minimize the greatness of God, while mentally maximizing the supposed greatness of Satan. In other words, Satan wants us to think he is greater than God."

Beloved, the time has come to turn the tables on the enemy of the church by undertaking a fresh study of the character of God for the primary purpose of enriching our praises of Him. And as we do, may we set new praise goals—

goals that mirror the heart cry of the sixteenth-century monk, Brother Lawrence, who wrote, "The thing we ought to purpose to ourselves in this life is to become the most perfect worshipper of God we can possibly be, as we hope to be through all eternity."[41]

Part 2

The Content of Our Praise

In order to heighten the focus of the various potential points for praise, I have chosen to provide a more substantive meditation on the first word used to praise God each week. This can serve as a pattern for readers to discover and develop for themselves the potential significance of the various qualities on each weekly list. Eventually, this seven-week list may well become a *seven-day list,* thus saturating each week in God's nature and character as you spend time faithfully in prayer and praise.

Week One

Amazed at God's Love

Your unfailing love is better to me than life itself; how I praise you!

Psalm 63:3

The love of God, the first of seven "ways of praise" assigned to week one's list, is an excellent starting point for any systematic program of praise. It is difficult to know which aspect of God's character or nature should be treated first. Few followers of Jesus would argue that were it not for God's love, little would matter in compiling any such praise lists. It is, quite simply, the love of God that draws mankind to explore His character and nature in the first place. Thus, to praise effectively we begin by standing amazed at God's abounding love!

In addressing the subject of God's attributes, and particularly that of His love, John Bisagno states, "We cannot understand who God is without understanding what God is like. And we cannot understand what God is like without understanding the characteristics of God, especially the love of God."[1]

The Significance of God's Love

God's love is clearly foundational to all that God is. Try to fathom for a moment an almighty, all-powerful God bent on evil and not on love. How infinitely important is that quality of God's essence we define as love! Bisagno states, "If we fail to understand that God is a God of love, we fail to grasp the full meaning of His personality. Without a doctrine of God's love, we are lost in our quest to understand the full dimensions of God's grandeur, His sovereignty, His immutability, His glory, and His majesty. The irrepressible power of God is cast in the characteristic of love."[2]

Bisagno beautifully concludes, "Love is like the glue that binds together the other personality characteristics of God and gives them a sharper, clearer meaning and focus."[3]

It also is significant that any nice qualities about us do not particularly stir God to love us, but rather He simply is love. He cannot *not* love us because His very essence is love.

Generally speaking, our tendency is to love someone who shows us kindness or to love someone to whom we are attracted in some way. God's love, however, is absolute, immutable and self-sufficient. It exists in and by itself and cannot change. James I. Packer emphasizes, "We do not make friends with *God; God* makes friends with *us*, bringing us to know Him by making His love known to us."[4]

The Power of God's Love

Love, further, is power. It can unite, heal and soothe as well as create a climate of joy and peace. And because God is infinite in His power as well as in His love, His love is infinitely powerful. God's love, indeed, touches every aspect of our lives. A. W. Tozer states, "Love wills the good of all and never wills harm or evil to any. This explains the words of the apostle John: 'There is no fear in love; but perfect love casteth out fear . . .' (1 John 4:18)."

He adds, "To know that love is of God and to enter into the secret place leaning upon the arm of the Beloved—this and only this can cast out fear. Let a man become convinced that nothing can harm him and instantly for him all fear goes out of the universe."[5]

Praise the Lord! Nothing in the entire universe can become an object of fear—*if* we are filled with God, for God is love. So, to be filled with love, we must be filled with God. And to be filled with God's love replaces even the possibility of fear. How rich is the power of God's infinite love!

The Extent of God's Love

To say that God is all in all is to say that God's attributes are all in all. His love, then, is all that love can possibly be—the absolute highest quality of love. And because God is altogether omnipresent—meaning all that God is, is always and everywhere present—the whole universe is filled with His love.

The extent of God's love is well summarized by Tozer: "From God's other known attributes we may learn much about His love. We can know, for instance, that because God is self-existent, His love had no beginning; because He is eternal, His love can have no end; because He is infinite, it has no limit; because He is holy, it has the quintessence of all spotless purity; because He is immense, His love is an incomprehensibly vast, bottomless, shoreless sea before which we kneel in joyful silence and from which the loftiest eloquence retreats confused and abashed."[6]

Packer adds: "The measure of love is how much it gives, and the measure of the love of God is the gift of His only

Son to be made man, and to die for sins, and so to become the One mediator who can bring us to God."[7]

The Prominence of God's Love

At one time or another as we approach the subject of the existence of a Supreme Being, we find ourselves asking the simple question—"Who is God?" The Bible provides three very specific answers: first, "For God is Spirit, so those who worship him must worship in spirit and in truth" (John 4:24); second, "God is light and there is no darkness in him at all" (1 John 1:5b); and third, "God is love" (1 John 4:8b).

Commenting on this threefold biblical analysis, Bisagno states, "These three characteristics—spirit, light, and love—answer the question, 'Who is God?' These three attributes of God provide the basis for our doctrine of God. God is spirit; God is light; God is love. Fully one-third of the nature of God is biblically described in terms of love."[8]

The Design of Love

Although God's love exists in and by itself, for God is love, it might be said that there is a design or purpose for God's love. Tozer expresses, "The love of God is one of the great realities of the universe, a pillar upon which the hope of the world rests. But it is a personal, intimate thing, too. God does not love populations, He loves people. He loves not masses, but men."[9]

God's love, then, must not be viewed purely as an impersonal quality of His nature that is diluted in generalities but as a quality that touches very specific individual lives. God's love is clearly a *personal* thing. True, God *does* love men, but more than that, He loves you and me and *every* human being individually.

How might God's love further be defined? James Orr states: "Love, generally, is that principle which leads one moral being to desire and delight in another, and reaches its highest form in that personal fellowship in which each lives in the life of the other, and finds his joy in imparting himself to the other, and in receiving back the outflow of that other's affection unto himself."

Tozer expands our definition: "Another characteristic of love is that it takes pleasure in its object. God enjoys His creation. The apostle John says frankly that God's purpose in creation was His own pleasure (Rev. 4:11). God is happy in His love for all that He has made."[10]

What a joy it is to know God loves us. Packer suggests, "There is tremendous relief in knowing that His love to me is utterly realistic, based at every point on prior knowledge of the worst about me, so that no discovery now can disillusion Him about me, in the way I am so often disillusioned about myself, and quench His determination to bless me."[11]

Here is an unfathomable mystery: God chose me to be His friend. And He also chose you. Imagine, an infinitely eternal Being, who needs nothing to enhance His essence or satisfaction, chose to call us "friends." Tozer expresses, "It is a strange and beautiful eccentricity of the free God that He has allowed His heart to be emotionally identified with men. Self-sufficient as He is, He wants our love and will not be satisfied till He gets it. Free as He is, He has let His heart be bound to us forever. 'This is real love. It is not that we loved God, but that he loved us and sent his Son as a sacrifice to take away our sins' (1 John 4:10)."[12]

Thus, the sum total of all that we might seek in understanding the attributes of God is that we might understand His love. "Let me seek Thee in longing," declared Anselm, "let me long for Thee in seeking; let me find Thee in love, and love Thee in finding."[13]

Sunday

Father God . . . You are—LOVING!

LOVE: Strong affection and passionate devotion, characterized by fondness, regard and enjoyment toward the object of one's love.

Lord, the foundation of Your very existence is love. I rejoice in the realization that You take enjoyment in loving me. I am overwhelmed that I am the object of Your strong affection and passionate devotion.
Your Word declares . . .

Can anything ever separate us from Christ's love? Does it mean he no longer loves us if we have trouble or calamity, or are persecuted, or are hungry or cold or in danger or threatened with death? (Even the Scriptures say, "For your sake we are killed every day; we are being slaughtered like sheep.") No, despite all these things, overwhelming victory is ours through Christ, who loved us.

And I am convinced that nothing can ever separate us from his love. Death can't, and life can't. The angels can't, and the demons can't. Our fears for today, our worries about tomorrow, and even the powers of hell can't keep God's love away. Whether we are high above the sky or in the deepest ocean, nothing in all creation will ever be able to separate us from the love of God that is revealed in Christ Jesus our Lord.

Romans 8:35–39

Long ago the LORD said to Israel: "I have loved you, my people, with an everlasting love. With unfailing love I have drawn you to myself."

Jeremiah 31:3

But God is so rich in mercy, and he loved us so very much, that even while we were dead because of our sins, he gave us life when he raised Christ from the dead.

Ephesians 2:4–5

Related references—Romans 5:8–10; 1 John 4:7–8.
Lord . . . I Praise Your LOVE!

Monday

Father God . . . You are—TIMELESS!

TIMELESS: That which continues endlessly in time. Not limited or affected by the restraint of time. Unending and eternal. Without duration and absent of the restrictions associated with time.

Lord, You are not limited or affected by the confines or restrictions of time. I rejoice in Your eternal endlessness. Because You are without beginning or ending and absent of all restrictions of time, You are never in a hurry to accomplish Your purpose.
Your Word declares . . .

"I, even I, am the LORD, and apart from me there is no savior. I have revealed and saved and proclaimed—I, and not some foreign god among you. You are my witnesses," declares the LORD, "that I am God. Yes, and from ancient days I am he. No one can deliver out of my hand. When I act, who can reverse it?"

Isaiah 43:11–13 NIV

And God has also commanded that the heavens and the earth will be consumed by fire on the day of judgment, when ungodly people will perish.
But you must not forget, dear friends, that a day is like a thousand years to the Lord, and a thousand years is like a day.

2 Peter 3:7–8

Understand, therefore, that the LORD your God is indeed God. He is the faithful God who keeps his covenant for a thousand generations and constantly loves those who love him and obey his commands.

Deuteronomy 7:9

Lord . . . I Praise Your TIMELESSNESS!

Tuesday

Father God . . . You are—PRESENT!

PRESENT: That which has its existence in the present. To be currently in view or at hand; close, near and immediate.

Lord, no matter where I go, You are already there. I glory in the reality of Your unfathomable nearness. With every trial that I face, I joyfully discover You have gone before me to guide me. You are truly the God of the now!
Your Word declares . . .

Where can I go from your Spirit? Where can I flee from your presence? If I go up to the heavens, you are there; if I make my bed in the depths, you are there. If I rise on the wings of the dawn, if I settle on the far side of the sea, even there your hand will guide me, your right hand will hold me fast.

Psalm 139:7–10 NIV

When you go out to fight your enemies and you face horses and chariots and an army greater than your own, do not be afraid. The LORD your God, who brought you safely out of Egypt, is with you! . . . Do not be afraid as you go out to fight today! Do not lose heart or panic. For the LORD your God is going with you! He will fight for you against your enemies, and he will give you victory!

Deuteronomy 20:1, 3–4

I will go before you, Cyrus, and level the mountains. I will smash down gates of bronze and cut through bars of iron. And I will give you treasures hidden in the darkness—secret riches. I will do this so you may know that I am the LORD, the God of Israel, the one who calls you by name.

Isaiah 45:2–3

My Presence will go with you, and I will give you rest.

Exodus 33:14 NIV

Yet I am always with you; you hold me by my right hand. You guide me with your counsel, and afterward you will take me into glory.

Psalm 73:23–24 NIV

Lord . . . I Praise Your PRESENCE!

Wednesday

Father God . . . You are—UNIQUE!

UNIQUE: Being one of a kind. Different from all others. Having no like or equal. Unparalleled and matchless.

Lord, You are absolutely unparalleled in Your splendor and matchless in Your essence. I take joy in praising Your uniqueness. You are different from all others; You have no like or equal.
Your Word declares . . .

My heart rejoices in the LORD! Oh, how the LORD has blessed me! Now I have an answer for my enemies, as I delight in your deliverance.
No one is holy like the LORD! There is no one besides you; there is no Rock like our God.

1 Samuel 2:1–2

Oh, the joys of those who trust the LORD, who have no confidence in the proud, or in those who worship idols.
O LORD my God, you have done many miracles for us. Your plans for us are too numerous to list. If I tried to recite all your wonderful deeds, I would never come to the end of them.

Psalm 40:4–5

And do not forget the things I have done throughout history. For I am God—I alone! I am God, and there is no one else like me. Only I can tell you what is going to happen even before it happens. Everything I plan will come to pass, for I do whatever I wish.

Isaiah 46:9–10

Related references—1 Corinthians 15:26–28; Colossians 1:17–18; 2 Samuel 7:22.

Lord . . . I Praise Your UNIQUENESS!

Thursday

Father God . . . You are—SPOTLESS!

SPOTLESS: Existing in a state of absolute purity. Absent of any stain, blemish or contamination. Stainless and pure. Immaculate.

Lord, with delight I acknowledge Your absolute purity. You are free of all contamination and unmarked by any stain. You are without spot or blemish and I glory in the liberating power of Your immaculate purity.
Your Word declares . . .

For you know that God paid a ransom to save you from the empty life you inherited from your ancestors. And the ransom he paid was not mere gold or silver. He paid for you with the precious lifeblood of Christ, the sinless, spotless Lamb of God.

1 Peter 1:18–19

That is why we have a great High Priest who has gone to heaven, Jesus the Son of God. Let us cling to him and never stop trusting him. This High Priest of ours understands our weaknesses, for he faced all of the same temptations we do, yet he did not sin. So let us come boldly to the throne of our gracious God. There we will receive his mercy, and we will find grace to help us when we need it.

Hebrews 4:14–16

And remember, no one who wants to do wrong should ever say, "God is tempting me." God is never tempted to do wrong, and he never tempts anyone else either.

James 1:13

Lord . . . I Praise Your SPOTLESSNESS!

Friday

Father God . . . You are—GLORIOUS!

GLORIOUS: Possessing or deserving of glory and praise. Praiseworthy, delightful and resplendent. Exalted, esteemed and eminent.

Lord, with my words I exalt You, and with my lips I esteem Your glory. I declare that You are worthy of honor and praise. All that You are is glorious, deserving of worship. I rejoice in Your resplendent magnificence.
Your Word declares . . .

God is well known in Judah; his name is great in Israel. . . . You are glorious and more majestic than the everlasting mountains.

Psalm 76:1, 4

I will meditate on your majestic, glorious splendor and your wonderful miracles. Your awe-inspiring deeds will be on every tongue; I will proclaim your greatness.

Psalm 145:5–6

Riches and honor come from you alone, for you rule over everything. Power and might are in your hand, and it is at your discretion that people are made great and given strength.
O our God, we thank you and praise your glorious name!

1 Chronicles 29:12–13

Bless the LORD God, the God of Israel, who alone does such wonderful things. Bless his glorious name forever! Let the whole earth be filled with his glory. Amen and amen!

Psalm 72:18–19

I will proclaim the name of the LORD; how glorious is our God!

He is the Rock; his work is perfect. Everything he does is just and fair. He is a faithful God who does no wrong; how just and upright he is!

Deuteronomy 32:3–4

Lord . . . I Praise Your GLORY!

Saturday

Father God . . . You are—GREAT!

GREAT: That which is eminent and grand; markedly superior in quality or skill. To be unrivaled, exceptional, surpassing and renowned. To be remarkable or outstanding in magnitude, degree or extent. Superior in quality or character; noble; excellent.

Lord, my lips declare Your absolute eminence. You are remarkable in quality and outstanding in character. I praise Your magnificent excellence and glory in Your awesome greatness.

Your Word declares . . .

I pray that you will begin to understand the incredible greatness of his power for us who believe him. This is the same mighty power that raised Christ from the dead and seated him in the place of honor at God's right hand in the heavenly realms.

Ephesians 1:19–20

I will praise you, my God and King, and bless your name forever and ever. I will bless you every day, and I will praise you forever. Great is the LORD! He is most worthy of praise! His greatness is beyond discovery!

Psalm 145:1–3

All the nations—and you made each one—will come and bow before you, Lord; they will praise your great and holy name. For you are great and perform great miracles. You alone are God.

Psalm 86:9–10

Come, let us sing to the LORD! Let us give a joyous shout to the rock of our salvation! Let us come before him with thanksgiving. Let us sing him psalms of praise. For the LORD is a great God, the great King above all gods. He owns the depths of the earth, and even the mightiest mountains are his.

Psalm 95:1–4

Lord . . . I Praise Your GREATNESS!

Summary for Week One

Father God, You are . . .
    LOVING,
        TIMELESS,
            PRESENT
                and UNIQUE;
    SPOTLESS,
        GLORIOUS
            and GREAT!

Week Two

Amazed at God's Holiness

Who will not fear, O Lord, and glorify your name? For you
alone are holy.

Revelation 15:4

৯৬৯

Few themes are more important to our understanding of
true worship than the theme of God's holiness. Frequently
the Bible pictures God as "the Holy One." Arthur W. Pink
explains, "God only is independently, infinitely, and
immutably holy. He is absolute Purity, unsullied even by
the shadow of sin."[1]

Steven Charnock's classic analysis of the character of
God, published three hundred years ago, contains this
description of God's holiness: "Chief emphasis is placed
upon this perfection of God; God is oftener styled Holy
than Almighty, and set forth by this part of His dignity more
than by any other. You never find it expressed, 'His mighty
name' or 'His wise name,' but 'His great name,' and most
of all, 'His holy name.' This is the greatest honor: in this
latter doth the majesty and venerableness of His name
appear."[2]

The absolute necessity of God's infinite holiness is perhaps best summed up in Jack Hayford's words, "God's holi-

ness is that attribute of God by which He preserves or retains the integrity of His entire being." As we come closer to God in practical praise, may we increasingly stand amazed at His absolute holiness.

The Source of God's Holiness

To finite man, holiness implies what might be termed "acquired perfection," or the reaching of a state of purity by taking certain steps that lead to spiritual maturity. But with God, holiness is not a growth process but an unqualified, ongoing reality. His holiness simply flows out of the absolute purity of His essence. Holy is simply how He is! John Bisagno declares, "God's holiness is not derived from another person, nor is it self-initiated or self-actuated. God did not acquire His holiness by man's decree or by heaven's ordination. He did not, at some point in His existence, decide to become holy. God, who is the great 'I AM,' possesses qualities of His nature which are eternal. Being holy is intrinsically, innately, inherently, and eternally a part of His nature."[3]

A. W. Tozer amplifies this thought, "Holy is the way God is. To be holy He does not conform to a standard. He is absolutely holy with an infinite, incomprehensible fullness of purity that is incapable of being other than it is. Because He is holy, all His attributes are holy; that is, whatever we think of as belonging to God must be thought of as holy."[4] Pink adds, "Nothing but that which is excellent can proceed from Him. Holiness is the rule of all His actions."[5]

William B. Pope further contributes, "After all that has been said as to the foundation of goodness and the reason why good is good, we are shut up to one view only. God alone is holy; not because He submits to a law binding on Him and on us all; but because holiness has its eternal standard and sanction in Him. God's nature is the sum and the standard of all goodness; and it is eternally opposed to all that is not good."[6]

The Meaning of God's Holiness

Before we further evaluate God's holiness, a pause for a stricter definition may be beneficial. Tozer responds, "God is holy and He has made holiness the moral condition necessary to the health of His universe. Sin's temporary presence in the world only accents this. Whatever is holy is healthy; evil is a moral sickness that must end ultimately in death. The formation of the language itself suggests this, the English word 'holy' deriving from the Anglo-Saxon 'halig,' 'hal,' meaning 'well, whole.'"[7]

That which is holy, then, is that which is whole, or complete. It is that which is well. Herman Bavinck states, "Holiness means separateness. The term is used with reference to persons or things which have been separated, or set apart (especially for God's service)."[8] The author expands his definition, "The Hebrew root *gdsh* is usually derived from the root *gd*, meaning to cut, to separate, hence it indicates apartness, separateness. The word holy is used first of all with reference to all kinds of persons and things which have been separated from their ordinary sphere, and placed in a peculiar relation to God and to His service."[9]

Holiness, then, refers simply to that which is free from every stain. It is that which exists in absolute purity. It is a word difficult to comprehend in human terms because we lack adequate models, or examples, with which to define it.

Bisagno evaluates this enigma: "The word that is translated 'holy' and 'holiness' in our English Bible comes from a Hebrew word that is impossible to define from its component parts. In most Greek or Hebrew words, we may take the sum of the parts comprising the finished word and learn its meaning. But the definition of 'holy' cannot come from the Hebrew. The Hebrew definition can only describe the act or character of something or someone that is holy. To grasp the full meaning of holiness then, is to describe, not to define. It is interesting that our Lord so structured the word that it defies definition."[10]

Bavinck provides a further clarification of this quality of God's essence. He writes, "When the word holy is ascribed to Jehovah, it does not signify one definite attribute. On the contrary, God is called holy in a very general sense: in connection with every revelation which impresses man with God's exalted majesty. Holiness is synonymous with divinity. . . . God's holiness is revealed in His entire relation to His people."[11] The theologian adds, "The same holiness which is the principle of redemption and object of praise, is for the transgressors the principle of their destruction and object of fear. In the latter case holy is synonymous with jealous."[12]

The wrath of God, then, is actually the outflow of His holiness. His holiness, in a sense, necessitates His strong revulsion to sin. Tozer writes, "Since God's first concern for His universe is its moral health, that is, its holiness, whatever is contrary to this is necessarily under His eternal displeasure. To preserve His creation God must destroy whatever would destroy it. When He arises to put down iniquity and save the world from irreparable moral collapse, He is said to be angry. Every wrathful judgment in the history of the world has been a holy act of preservation. The holiness of God, the wrath of God, and the health of the creation are inseparably united. God's wrath is utter intolerance of whatever degrades and destroys. He hates iniquity as a mother hates the polio that would take the life of her child."[13]

Suddenly we see God's wrath from a different perspective. The purity of His essence, which we call His holiness, requires it. Pink explains, "Because God is holy He *hates all sin*. He loves everything which is in conformity to His law, and loathes everything which is contrary to it. His Word plainly declares, 'The forward is abomination to the LORD' (Prov. 3:32). And again, 'The thoughts of the wicked are an abomination to the LORD' (Prov. 15:26)." He concludes, "God has often forgiven sinners, but He never forgives sin; and the sinner is only forgiven on the ground of another having borne his punishment; for 'without shedding of blood is no remission' (Heb. 9:22)."[14]

God's holiness, then, categorically declares God's entire nature as being universally opposed to evil. True, He is loving, and He is *the* essence of love. But this does not mean He will love sin. Bisagno explains, "God's holiness acts as a balance to other aspects of His nature, including His characteristic of love. Though He is a God of love, the Lord is constrained to set Himself completely against sin and sinners. Everything that God has created is set in motion against sin."[15]

The Application of God's Holiness

Because God tells us in His Word to "be holy because I am holy" (1 Peter 1:16), we really need a meaningful understanding of what it means to apply God's holiness to our everyday growth in Christ. Herman Bavinck shares, "Whatever is holy lives a peculiar life, bears a peculiar character, has been separated from the common sphere and from the common law, that is, it may not be touched . . . it may not be eaten . . . it may not be used."[16] The suggestion is that to be filled with the God who is absolutely holy is to manifest at least some of those qualities that arise from His holiness. Bavinck adds, "Holy is whatever has been chosen and set apart by Jehovah, has been deprived of the character which it possessed in common with other things, and has by means of special ceremonies been given a distinctive character so that it is now living in this new condition in accordance with those laws which have been prescribed for it."[17]

Thus, the holiness of God must affect our very manner of life. Bisagno points out, "God demands a life that presses on toward perfection. The holiness of God should attract us toward God, not pull us away from Him."[18]

The Importance of God's Holiness

Because God's attributes describe all that God is, it is difficult to determine if any particular attribute is more significant than any other. Still, God's holiness appears to have a special prominence on the list. In a sense, many other attributes flow from it. Consider, for example, the unique fact that twice in the Scriptures angels are discovered using this specific attribute as their foundational word for worship: once in the Old Testament and once in the New. Isaiah tells of angelic beings declaring, "Holy, holy, holy is the LORD Almighty! The whole earth is filled with his glory" (Isa. 6:3). John's Revelation shows these creatures of worship proclaiming, "Holy, holy, holy is the Lord God Almighty—the one who always was, who is, and who is still to come" (Rev. 4:8). William B. Pope declares, "It is obvious in these passages to observe how strong confirmation this gives to the doctrine of the Holy Trinity: of all God's attributes this is the only thrice-uttered perfection."[19]

Pope probes the significance of the biblical treatment of God's holiness further and adds, "The Son addresses the 'Holy Father'; He is Himself as Incarnate, the 'Holy Child' while the Spirit of God is 'The Holy Ghost.'"[20] He concludes, "It is plain that throughout the Old Testament the holiness and the mercy of God are supreme: on these two hang all the redeeming attributes."[21]

Thus, the importance of God's holiness cannot be overstated. In fact, spiritual leaders in ancient Israel actually appointed singers specifically for "praising him for his holy splendor" (2 Chron. 20:21), a thought that prompted Steven Charnock three centuries ago to write, "Power is God's hand or arm, omniscience His eye, mercy His bowels, eternity His duration, *but holiness is His beauty.*"[22]

A. W. Tozer adds powerfully, "God is the absolute quintessence of moral excellence, infinitely perfect in righteousness, purity, rectitude and incomprehensible holiness. And in all this He is uncreated, self-sufficient and beyond the power of human thought to conceive or human speech to utter."[23]

Indeed, God's holiness is not only important, but it might be viewed as the very starting point for evaluating the totality of God's character. John Bisagno states, "Any study of God's characteristics must logically begin with a look at the holiness of God, because more than any other attribute, God's holiness is what sets Him apart from man."[24]

The Uniqueness of God's Holiness

God's characteristics might be termed "unique," in that each aspect is one-of-a-kind. However, we find ourselves describing God's holiness as being uniquely unique. It truly is beyond explanation. Tozer suggests,

> We cannot grasp the true meaning of divine holiness by thinking of someone or something very pure and then raising the concept to the highest degree we are capable of. God's holiness is not simply the best we know infinitely bettered. We know nothing like the divine holiness. It stands apart, unique, unapproachable, incomprehensible and unattainable. The natural man is blind to it. He may fear God's power and admire His wisdom, but His holiness he cannot even imagine. Only the Spirit of the Holy One can impart to the human spirit the knowledge of the Holy.[25]

In a theological treatise published almost one century ago, William B. Pope provides further insight into the uniqueness of God's holiness: "As God is the Being of Beings, His supreme perfection is the perfection of all perfections. The perfection we reverently ascribe to God is unique, and excludes the possibility of defect; it is supreme and immutable, not the finish of a process; it is the ground and standard and source of all other perfection."[26]

How might we sum up this awesome attribute of God? In 1670 John Howe wrote, "God's holiness may be said to be a transcendental attribute, that, as it were, runs throughout the rest, and casts luster upon them. It is the attribute of attributes."[27]

No finer conclusion to this overview of God's holiness can be found than this evaluation, published in 1682 by Steven Charnock:

> God's holiness seems to challenge an excellency above all His other perfections, so it is the glory of all the rest: as it is the glory of the Godhead, so it is the glory of every perfection in the Godhead; as His power is the strength of Him, so His holiness is the beauty of them; as all His characteristics would be weak without almightiness to back them, so all would be uncomely without holiness to adorn them. Should this be sullied, all the rest would lose their honor; as at the same instant the sun should lose its sight, it would lose its heat, its strength, its generative and quickening virtue. As sincerity is the luster of every grace in a Christian, so is purity the splendor of every attribute in the Godhead. His justice is a holy justice, His wisdom a holy wisdom, His arm of power a "holy arm" (Ps. 98:1), His truth or promise a "holy promise" (Ps. 105:42); His name which signifies all His attributes in conjunction, "is holy" (Ps. 103:1).[28]

Praise God for His infinite holiness!

Sunday

Father God . . . You are—HOLY!

HOLY: Existing in a state of absolute spiritual perfection and purity. Faultless and undefiled in nature and character; thoroughly clean. That which is absolutely righteous.

Lord, with my lips I acknowledge Your absolute holiness. You are faultless and undefiled, clean in every way. I praise the totality of Your perfection and purity. You are altogether holy.

Your Word declares . . .

In the year King Uzziah died, I saw the Lord. He was sitting on a lofty throne, and the train of his robe filled the Temple. Hovering around him were mighty seraphim, each with six wings. With two wings they covered their faces, with two they covered their feet, and with the remaining two they flew. In a great chorus they sang, "Holy, holy, holy is the LORD Almighty! The whole earth is filled with his glory!"

Isaiah 6:1–3

Who will not fear, O Lord, and glorify your name? For you alone are holy. All nations will come and worship before you, for your righteous deeds have been revealed.

Revelation 15:4

Who else among the gods is like you, O LORD? Who is glorious in holiness like you—so awesome in splendor, performing such wonders?

Exodus 15:11

The LORD is king! Let the nations tremble! He sits on his throne between the cherubim. Let the whole earth quake! . . . Exalt the LORD our God and worship at his holy mountain in Jerusalem, for the LORD our God is holy!

Psalm 99:1, 9

But mightier than the violent raging of the seas, mightier than the breakers on the shore—the LORD above is mightier than these! Your royal decrees cannot be changed. The nature of your reign, O LORD, is holiness forever.

Psalm 93:4–5

Related references—Isaiah 57:15; Psalm 22:2–3; 1 Chronicles 16:8–10.

Lord . . . I Praise Your HOLINESS!

Monday

Father God . . . You are—EXCELLENT!

EXCELLENT: The quality of representing that which is distinctive, superior and invaluable; the very finest and choicest. To be supreme and priceless.

Lord, with lips of joy I praise the absolute excellence of Your nature and character. You are truly distinctive, superior and invaluable in Your marvelous essence. You are priceless and supreme. I glory in Your excellence.
Your Word declares . . .

Happy art thou, O Israel: who is like unto thee, O people saved by the LORD, the shield of thy help, and who is the sword of thy excellency! And thine enemies shall be found liars unto thee; and thou shalt tread upon their high places.

Deuteronomy 33:29 KJV

As for the Almighty, we cannot find Him; He is excellent in power, in judgment and abundant justice; He does not oppress.

Job 37:23 NKJV

O LORD, our Lord, how excellent is Your name in all the earth, Who have set Your glory above the heavens.

Psalm 8:1 NKJV

Let them praise the name of the Lord: for his name alone is excellent; his glory is above the earth and heaven.

Psalm 148:13 KJV

Sing to the Lord, for He has done excellent things; this is known in all the earth. Cry out and shout, O inhabitant of Zion, for great is the Holy One of Israel in your midst!

Isaiah 12:5–6 NKJV

Lord . . . I Praise Your EXCELLENCE!

Tuesday

Father God . . . You are—RELIABLE!

RELIABLE: The nature or characteristic of one who can be trusted or is reliable. Unimpeachable, unequivocal and unquestionable. One who is steady, loyal and dependable.

Lord, with my words of praise I honor Your dependability and I glory in Your steadfastness and loyalty. You are unquestionable in Your decisions and unimpeachable in every action. I praise You, Lord, for You can be trusted! Your Word declares . . .

God is not a man, that he should lie, nor a son of man, that he should change his mind. Does he speak and then not act? Does he promise and not fulfill? I have received a command to bless; he has blessed, and I cannot change it.

Numbers 23:19–20 NIV

Stay away from the love of money; be satisfied with what you have. For God has said, "I will never fail you. I will never forsake you." That is why we can say with confidence, "The Lord is my helper, so I will not be afraid. What can mere mortals do to me?"

Hebrews 13:5–6

Praise the LORD who has given rest to his people Israel, just as he promised. Not one word has failed of all the wonderful promises he gave through his servant Moses.

1 Kings 8:56

Listen to me, all you who are left in Israel. I created you and have cared for you since before you were born. I will be your God throughout your lifetime—until your hair is white with age. I made you, and I will care for you. I will carry you along and save you.

Isaiah 46:3–4

Lord, you have been our dwelling place throughout all generations. Before the mountains were born or you brought forth the earth and the world, from everlasting to everlasting you are God.

Psalm 90:1–2 NIV

Lord . . . I Praise Your RELIABILITY!

Wednesday

Father God . . . You are—STRONG!

STRONG: The quality of possessing power to resist or endure an attack. To possess vigor and vitality, energy and intensity. That which is capable of enduring and able to withstand any assault.

Lord, Your essence abounds with vigor and vitality. I praise Your power and I glory in Your strength. Because You are infinitely strong, I dwell in the tabernacle of Your limitless power. In You only do I live and breathe and have my being.

Your Word declares . . .

God arms me with strength; he has made my way safe. He makes me as surefooted as a deer, leading me safely along the mountain heights. He prepares me for battle; he strengthens me to draw a bow of bronze.

Psalm 18:32–34

And he will stand to lead his flock with the LORD's strength, in the majesty of the name of the LORD his God. Then his people will live there undisturbed, for he will be highly honored all around the world.

Micah 5:4

"See, God has come to save me. I will trust in him and not be afraid. The LORD GOD is my strength and my song; he has become my salvation."

With joy you will drink deeply from the fountain of salvation!

Isaiah 12:2–3

The LORD is my strength and my song; he has become my victory. Songs of joy and victory are sung in the camp of the godly. The strong right arm of the LORD has done glorious things! The strong right arm of the LORD is raised in triumph. The strong right arm of the LORD has done glorious things!

Psalm 118:14–16

Lord . . . I Praise Your STRENGTH!

Thursday

Father God . . . You are—SUFFICIENT!

SUFFICIENT: Adequate for the meeting of any demand placed on a particular resource or supply. Existing in abundance in reference to any need. Having exactly enough, or more than enough, to meet all demands.

Lord, You are more than adequate for my every need. I rejoice in the abundance of Your supply. No demand could ever exhaust the infinite reservoir of Your goodness. You are the God who is enough!
Your Word declares . . .

Not that we are sufficient of ourselves to think of anything as being from ourselves, but our sufficiency is from God, who also made us sufficient as ministers of the new covenant, not of the letter but of the Spirit; for the letter kills, but the Spirit gives life.

2 Corinthians 3:5–6 NKJV

But he said to me, "My grace is sufficient for you, for my power is made perfect in weakness." Therefore I will boast all the more gladly about my weaknesses, so that Christ's power may rest on me. That is why, for Christ's sake, I delight in weaknesses, in insults, in hardships, in persecutions, in difficulties. For when I am weak, then I am strong.

2 Corinthians 12:9–10 NIV

And God is able to make all grace abound toward you, that you, always having all sufficiency in all things, may have an abundance for every good work.

2 Corinthians 9:8 NKJV

And my God will meet all your needs according to his glorious riches in Christ Jesus.

Philippians 4:19 NIV

The LORD your God has blessed everything you have done and has watched your every step through this great wilderness. During these forty years, the LORD your God has been with you and provided for your every need so that you lacked nothing.

Deuteronomy 2:7

Lord . . . I Praise Your SUFFICIENCY!

Friday

Father God . . . You are—MEASURELESS!

MEASURELESS: The absence of any restrictions placed on a resource. Incapable of being measured by any standard means of measuring areas of dimension, capacity, weight, mass or scope.

Lord, I declare that You are without measure in Your nature and character. You are incapable of being measured by any standard of measurement. Because You are measureless, Your attributes are limitless.

Your Word declares . . .

Look up into the heavens. Who created all the stars? He brings them out one after another, calling each by its name. And he counts them to see that none are lost or have strayed away.

O Israel, how can you say the LORD does not see your troubles? How can you say God refuses to hear your case? Have you never heard or understood? Don't you know that the LORD is the everlasting God, the Creator of all the earth? He never grows faint or weary. No one can measure the depths of his understanding.

Isaiah 40:26–28

For the LORD is a great God, the great King above all gods. He owns the depths of the earth, and even the mightiest mountains are his. The sea belongs to him, for he made it.

His hands formed the dry land, too. Come, let us worship and bow down. Let us kneel before the Lord our maker, for he is our God.

Psalm 95:3–7

"Stand up and praise the Lord your God, for he lives from everlasting to everlasting!"

Then they continued, "Praise his glorious name! It is far greater than we can think or say. You alone are the Lord. You made the skies and the heavens and all the stars. You made the earth and the seas and everything in them. You preserve and give life to everything, and all the angels of heaven worship you."

Nehemiah 9:5–6

Related references—Psalm 145:10, 13; Luke 1:37; 2 Chronicles 6:18; 1 Kings 8:27.

Lord . . . I Praise Your MEASURELESSNESS!

Saturday

Father God . . . You are—WISE!

WISE: Possessing qualities of intelligence, insight and good sense. Having at ready grasp philosophic or scientific knowledge, understanding and learning, with the capacity to properly apply that which is known.

Lord, all wisdom and understanding is the outflow of Your essence, for You are the fountainhead of all that can be known. I praise Your intelligence and I magnify Your knowledge. Your knowledge is infinite and Your wisdom supreme. You are truly the only wise God.
Your Word declares . . .

My child, listen to me and treasure my instructions. Tune your ears to wisdom, and concentrate on understanding. Cry out for insight and understanding. Search for them as you would for lost money or hidden treasure. Then you will understand what it means to fear the LORD, and you will gain knowledge of God. For the LORD grants wisdom! From his mouth come knowledge and understanding. He grants a treasure of good sense to the godly. He is their shield, protecting those who walk with integrity.

Proverbs 2:1–7

Listen to this, all you people! Pay attention, everyone in the world! High and low, rich and poor—listen! For my words are wise, and my thoughts are filled with insight.

Psalm 49:1–3

How we praise God, the Father of our Lord Jesus Christ, who has blessed us with every spiritual blessing in the heavenly realms because we belong to Christ. . . . He is so rich in kindness that he purchased our freedom through the blood of his Son, and our sins are forgiven. He has showered his kindness on us, along with all wisdom and understanding.

Ephesians 1:3, 7–8

Related references—Colossians 2:1–3; 1 Corinthians 1:24, 27.
Lord . . . I Praise Your WISDOM!

Summary for Week Two

Father God, You Are . . .
    HOLY,
        EXCELLENT,
           RELIABLE
               and STRONG;
    SUFFICIENT,
        MEASURELESS
           and WISE!

Week Three

Amazed at God's Majesty

Praise the Lord! . . . Praise him for his mighty works; praise his unequaled greatness!

Psalm 150:1–2

ﻌﻼ

As the elderly missionary lay motionless on her deathbed, her nine children gathered solemnly around her. Her life had been a long and beautiful example of dedication and sacrifice. All of her children followed in her footsteps and served in some aspect of missionary service.

Before a new day dawned the saintly warrior would be with Jesus, and everyone present knew death was moments away.

Suddenly, one of the children thought she heard her mother speak. It was unusual. It seemed like days since she had spoken. Motioning to the eldest son, the younger sister said, "I think Mother is trying to say something."

Her brother was certain it was but a groan, perhaps an indication that death had finally arrived. But a few seconds passed and it seemed that she again wanted to speak. This time what appeared to be a forced groan was clearly loud enough to be heard. Still, none could recognize what she wanted to say.

The eldest son put his ear close to his mother's lips and said, "Mother, please tell us what it is you want."

The dying saint struggled as she reached within for all the strength that remained. This time a clear word was heard: the single word—"Bring." There was no doubt about what she said.

The son leaned closer and spoke. "Mother," he said softly, "tell us what it is you wish. You name it and we will bring it to you."

The missionary's body seemed to quiver as she reached within for greater strength. "Bring," she cried out with authority.

Again the eldest son, longing to satisfy his dying mother's wish, responded, "Whatever it is you wish, Mother, just tell us. If we can possibly bring it to you, we will."

Almost interrupting the son, the mother cried even louder—"Bring!"

By now, the son seemed agitated and responded firmly, "Mother, just tell us what it is you want and we will bring it."

Suddenly, a remarkable thing happened. The saint seemed to burst forth with supernatural energy. Rising on her bed, an impossibility in her condition, she stretched a hand toward heaven and boldly exclaimed—*"Bring . . . forth the royal diadem and crown Him Lord of all!"*

With those words, the missionary fell backward on her pillow and died. She ended her earthly experience honoring the majesty of God.

Defining God's Majesty

When referring to the "majesty of God," we speak of God's divine splendor and supremacy as it relates to His kingly rule over the entire universe. James I. Packer explains: "Our word 'majesty' comes from the Latin; it means *greatness.* When we ascribe majesty to someone, we are acknowledging greatness in that person, and voicing our respect for it: as, for instance, when in England we speak of 'her majesty' the Queen."[1]

Scripture often uses the term *majesty* to describe the greatness of God. We read, "The LORD is king! He is robed in majesty. . . . Your throne, O LORD, has been established from time immemorial. You yourself are from the everlasting past" (Ps. 93:1–2). And, "I will meditate on your majestic, glorious splendor and your wonderful miracles" (Ps. 145:5). The apostle Peter, in writing of his experience on the Mount of Transfiguration, said, "We have seen his majestic splendor with our own eyes" (2 Peter 1:16).

Packer further suggests, "The word majesty, when we apply it to a discussion of God's character, is always a declaration of His greatness as well as an invitation to worship." Packer adds, "The same is true when the Bible speaks of God as being 'on high' and 'in heaven'; the thought here is not that God is far distant from us in space, but that He is far above us in greatness, and therefore to be adored."[2] To understand this is to stand amazed at the majesty of God.

Understanding God's Majesty

Just as God's holiness pictures the totality of His moral purity, His majesty portrays the totality of His eternal greatness. Herman Bavinck states, "There is no name or attribute which adequately expresses God's being; hence, many names or attributes serve the purpose of giving us an impression of His eminent majesty."[3] He adds, "God is the highest, best, most beautiful, most perfect essence . . . above Whom there is nothing, outside of Whom there is nothing, apart from Whom there is nothing. He is supreme life, supreme truth, supreme blessedness, supreme wisdom, and supreme essence."[4]

God's majesty, then, might be defined as the sum total of all His attributes. His love is majestic. His holiness is majestic. His mercy is majestic. Simply stated, He is the supreme King ruling over the entire universe. He is, indeed, *Lord of all.*

Arthur W. Pink, who interchanges the words *majesty* and *supremacy,* states, "God's supremacy over the works of His hands is vividly depicted in Scripture. Inanimate matter, irrational creatures, all perform their Maker's bidding. At His pleasure the Red Sea divided and its waters stood up as walls (Exod. 14); and the earth opened her mouth, and guilty rebels went live down into the pit (Num. 14). When God so ordered, the sun stood still (Josh. 10); and on another occasion went backward ten degrees on the dial of Ahaz (Isa. 38:8). To exemplify His supremacy, He made ravens carry food to Elijah (1 Kings 17), iron to swim on top of the water (2 Kings 6:5, 6), lions to be tamed when Daniel was cast into their den, fire to burn not when the three Hebrews were flung into its flames. Thus, 'Whatsoever the LORD pleased, that did he in heaven, and in earth, in the seas, and all deep places' (Ps. 135:6)."[5]

Recognizing God's Majesty

Because God's majesty is the totality of His greatness, it is a characteristic of God to be seen everywhere. Herman Bavinck states, "The entire universe reveals God: there is no atom of the universe which does not manifest something of His virtues."[6]

Sadly, some of us have failed to recognize the truth of God's awesome majesty. We are, perhaps, in need of a rebuke similar to that given by Martin Luther to Erasmus the monk, "Your thoughts of God are too human!"

In evaluating Luther's rebuke, Packer adds, "This is where most of us go astray. Our thoughts of God are not great enough; we fail to reckon with the reality of His limitless wisdom and power."[7]

God truly is great in majestic splendor whether we recognize it or not. And certainly our inability to acknowledge God in all His majesty does not lessen it. A. W. Tozer aptly advises, "Were all human beings suddenly to become blind, still the sun would shine by day and the stars by night, for these owe nothing to the millions who benefit from their light. So, were every man on earth to become an atheist, it could not affect God in any way. He is what He is in Himself without regard to any other. To believe in Him adds nothing to His perfections; to doubt Him takes nothing away."[8]

Indeed, the universe's myriad number of spiraling and expanding galaxies, with their star systems that some scientists estimate in the trillions, declares the majestic power of an infinitely majestic God. In the biblical chronicles of the ancient kings, we read, "Yours, O Lord, is the greatness, the power, the glory, the victory, and the majesty. Everything in the heavens and on earth is yours, O Lord, and this is your kingdom. We adore you as the one who is over all things. . . . for you rule over everything" (1 Chron. 29:11–12).

Contemplating God's Majesty

An article in *National Geographic,* which fails to mention that God was in any sense instrumental in the process of creation, seems to substantiate more than ever the majesty of God. The author takes the reader back to the very beginning of creation—at least as some scientists might define it—and describes that infinitely small fraction of a second when it all might have begun: "The latest theories propose that at that moment [of creation] the universe—all the cosmos that we can observe—was condensed into a region much smaller than an atom. Matter, as we know it, did not exist yet. The universe was pure, pent-up, exquisitely hot energy."[9]

Think of it! Some scientists believe that at a particular point in the almost infinite past everything that exists today—all the myriad star systems with their planets, including our sun, and even the substance that makes up the very walls of the room in which you may be sitting as you read this—was compressed into an area *smaller* than the size of a tiny atom. Amazingly, it contained an amount of substance that existed in a state of such intense heat that it exploded in an event termed "the big bang."

"What caused the big bang?" asks the author. "That question also still transcends our knowledge of physics." He adds, "However, a provocative new theory called the 'inflationary universe' takes us to that brink of our origin."

The author then quotes Alan Guth of the Massachusetts Institute of Technology, the originator of the theory, who says, "The inflationary universe attempts to build the universe from almost nothing."

Of course, those who recognize the majestic power of God have little difficulty going beyond this MIT professor in saying that God *did,* in actuality, create everything *from* nothing—not from "almost nothing."

Interestingly, the author later quotes Michael Turner, a University of Chicago physicist: "To get a universe that has expanded as long as ours has without either collapsing or having its matter coast away would have required extraordinary fine-tuning."

Without suggesting who might have been around to do the fine-tuning, the scientist adds, "The odds of achieving that kind of precise expansion . . . would be the same as throwing an imaginary microscopic dart across the universe to the most distant quasar and hitting a bull's-eye one millimeter in diameter."[10]

All of this serves to illustrate afresh the vastness of God's glorious majesty. It almost prompts one to shout in praise the verse by Frederick W. Faber:

> One God! One Majesty!
> There is no God but Thee!
> Unbounded, unextended unity!

Sunday

Father God . . . You are—MAJESTIC!

MAJESTIC: To possess or demonstrate qualities associated with royalty, dignity and sovereign grandeur. To exist in kingly splendor and greatness. To be illustrious and exalted.

Lord, I rejoice in Your majestic splendor. With my lips I honor Your sovereign grandeur and eternal dignity. You are both the King of the universe and the King of my life. My spirit bows humbly before Your greatness.
Your Word declares . . .

Put on your sword, O mighty warrior! You are so glorious, so majestic! In your majesty, ride out to victory, defending truth, humility, and justice. Go forth to perform awe-inspiring deeds! . . .
Your throne, O God, endures forever and ever. Your royal power is expressed in justice.

Psalm 45:3–4, 6

For we were not making up clever stories when we told you about the power of our Lord Jesus Christ and his coming again. We have seen his majestic splendor with our own eyes.

2 Peter 1:16

The LORD is king! He is robed in majesty. Indeed, the LORD is robed in majesty and armed with strength. The world is firmly established; it cannot be shaken. Your throne, O LORD, has been established from time immemorial. You yourself are from the everlasting past.

Psalm 93:1–2

The voice of the LORD echoes above the sea. The God of glory thunders. The LORD thunders over the mighty sea. The voice of the LORD is powerful; the voice of the LORD is full of majesty.

Psalm 29:3–4

Lord . . . I Praise Your MAJESTY!

Monday

Father God . . . You are—CREATIVE!

CREATIVE: The ability to cause to exist and to bring into being. The capacity to originate, generate, shape, form or cause something to become a reality.

Lord, I praise the creativity of Your divine nature for it has given birth to all creation. Through Your creative energy I have been formed, that I might be to You an everlasting song of rejoicing.

Your Word declares . . .

For the LORD is God, and he created the heavens and earth and put everything in place. He made the world to be lived in, not to be a place of empty chaos.

"I am the LORD," he says, "and there is no other."

Isaiah 45:18

Christ is the visible image of the invisible God. He existed before God made anything at all and is supreme over all creation. Christ is the one through whom God created everything in heaven and earth. He made the things we can see and the things we can't see—kings, kingdoms, rulers, and authorities. Everything has been created through him and for him. He existed before everything else began, and he holds all creation together.

Colossians 1:15–17

Listen to me, . . . I alone am God, the First and the Last. It was my hand that laid the foundations of the earth. The palm of my right hand spread out the heavens above. I spoke, and they came into being.

Isaiah 48:12–13

Related references—Isaiah 40:26–28; Revelation 10:5–6; Romans 4:16–17.

Lord . . . I Praise Your CREATIVITY!

Tuesday

Father God . . . You are—AVAILABLE!

AVAILABLE: The quality of being present, reachable and dependable when needed. That which is ready for use at any moment or any occasion.

Lord, I praise Your constant dependability, for it assures me You are there when I call. Because You are available, my spirit is comfortable. There is no danger ever so near that You are not nearer still. I glory in Your everlasting nearness!

Your Word declares . . .

God is our refuge and strength, always ready to help in times of trouble. So we will not fear, even if earthquakes come and the mountains crumble into the sea. Let the oceans roar and foam. Let the mountains tremble as the waters surge! . . . The Lord Almighty is here among us; the God of Israel is our fortress.

Psalm 46:1–3, 11

We thank you, O God! We give thanks because you are near. People everywhere tell of your mighty miracles.

Psalm 75:1

But you are near, O LORD, and all your commands are true. I have known from my earliest days that your decrees never change.

Psalm 119:151–52

Lord . . . I Praise Your AVAILABILITY!

Wednesday

Father God . . . You are—MIGHTY!

MIGHTY: Possessing the qualities of strength, power and authority. To exist in a state that is stalwart, extraordinary or monumental. To be very strong or great.

Lord, You are the great God, the God of might and power. I praise Your extraordinary strength and abounding authority. Your greatness is beyond measure and Your might is incomparable. You are, indeed, the mighty God! Your Word declares . . .

For the LORD will remove his hand of judgment and will disperse the armies of your enemy. And the LORD himself, the King of Israel, will live among you! At last your troubles will be over, and you will fear disaster no more.
    On that day the announcement to Jerusalem will be, "Cheer up, Zion! Don't be afraid! For the LORD your God has arrived to live among you. He is a mighty savior. He will rejoice over you with great gladness. With his love, he will calm all your fears. He will exult over you by singing a happy song."

Zephaniah 3:15–17

I pray that you will begin to understand the incredible greatness of his power for us who believe him. This is the same mighty power that raised Christ from the dead and seated him in the place of honor at God's right hand in the heavenly realms. Now he is far above any ruler or authority or power or leader or anything else in this world or in the world to come.

Ephesians 1:19–21

We are human, but we don't wage war with human plans and methods. We use God's mighty weapons, not mere worldly weapons, to knock down the Devil's strongholds. With these weapons we break down every proud argument that keeps people from knowing God. With these weapons we conquer their rebellious ideas, and we teach them to obey Christ.

2 Corinthians 10:3–5

For a child is born to us, a son is given to us. And the government will rest on his shoulders. These will be his royal titles: Wonderful Counselor, Mighty God, . . .

Isaiah 9:6

Lord . . . I Praise Your MIGHT!

Thursday

Father God . . . You are—STEADFAST!

STEADFAST: The quality of character that causes one to remain firmly loyal or constant; that which is unswerving, fixed, unchanging or steady.

Lord, because You are unchanging in Your nature, my spirit rejoices in steadfast confidence. You are firmly loyal and unswerving in the keeping of Your promises. I glory in Your everlasting steadiness.
Your Word declares . . .

Be strong and courageous! Do not be afraid of them! The LORD your God will go ahead of you. He will neither fail you nor forsake you. . . . Do not be afraid or discouraged, for the LORD is the one who goes before you. He will be with you; he will neither fail you nor forsake you.

Deuteronomy 31:6, 8

So the LORD gave to Israel all the land he had sworn to give their ancestors, and they conquered it and settled there. And the LORD gave them rest on every side, just as he had solemnly promised their ancestors. None of their enemies could stand against them, for the LORD helped them conquer all their enemies. All of the good promises that the LORD had given Israel came true.

Joshua 21:43–45

But I will never stop loving him, nor let my promise to him fail. No, I will not break my covenant; I will not take back a single word I said.

Psalm 89:33–34

Then David continued, "Be strong and courageous, and do the work. Don't be afraid or discouraged by the size of the task, for the Lord God, my God, is with you. He will not fail you or forsake you. He will see to it that all the work related to the Temple of the Lord is finished correctly."

1 Chronicles 28:20

Lord . . . I Praise Your STEADFASTNESS!

Friday

Father God . . . You are—GENEROUS!

GENEROUS: To be willing to give or share. The inclination toward or characteristic nature of an unselfish release of one's possessions to benefit others. A lack of pettiness or meanness in thought or behavior.

Lord, I praise Your unselfish generosity manifested in the release of Your only Son, Jesus Christ, to die on the cross for my redemption. With joy I worship Your unsparing willingness to share Your possessions with Your children.
Your Word declares . . .

He will bless those who fear the LORD, both great and small. May the LORD richly bless both you and your children. May you be blessed by the LORD, who made heaven and earth. The heavens belong to the LORD, but he has given the earth to all humanity.

Psalm 115:13–16

Be imitators of God, therefore, as dearly loved children, and live a life of love, just as Christ loved us and gave himself up for us as a fragrant offering and sacrifice to God.

Ephesians 5:1–2 NIV

May God bless you with his special favor and wonderful peace as you come to know Jesus, our God and Lord, better and better. As we know Jesus better, his divine power gives us everything we need for living a godly life. He has called us to receive his own glory and goodness!

2 Peter 1:2–3

If you need wisdom—if you want to know what God wants you to do—ask him, and he will gladly tell you. He will not resent your asking.

James 1:5 NIV

Related references—Matthew 7:7; Deuteronomy 8:18.
Lord . . . I Praise Your GENEROSITY!

Saturday

Father God . . . You are—ABLE!

ABLE: Having or possessing sufficient power, skill or resources to accomplish an objective. To be fitted or equipped for the demands of a specific task.

Lord, You are able to meet all my needs. I rejoice in Your ability and praise Your sufficiency. Because You are able, I am able, for I draw my strength from Your ability. Your Word declares . . .

Now glory be to God! By his mighty power at work within us, he is able to accomplish infinitely more than we would ever dare to ask or hope. May he be given glory in the church and in Christ Jesus forever and ever through endless ages. Amen.

Ephesians 3:20–21

For God has not given us a spirit of fear and timidity, but of power, love, and self-discipline. So you must never be ashamed to tell others about our Lord. And don't be ashamed of me, either, even though I'm in prison for Christ. With the strength God gives you, be ready to suffer with me for the proclamation of the Good News. . . . And that is why I am suffering here in prison. But I am not ashamed of it, for I know the one in whom I trust, and I am sure that he is able to guard what I have entrusted to him until the day of his return.

2 Timothy 1:7–8, 12

Therefore he is able, once and forever, to save everyone who comes to God through him. He lives forever to plead with God on their behalf.

Hebrews 7:25

Related reference—Philippians 3:20–21.
Lord . . . I Praise Your ABILITY!

Summary for Week Three

Father God, You Are . . .
    MAJESTIC,
        CREATIVE,
            AVAILABLE
                and MIGHTY;
    STEADFAST,
        GENEROUS
            and ABLE!

Week Four

Amazed at God's Justice

I will praise you seven times a day because all your laws
are just.

Psalm 119:164

ᏗᏯᎾ

Because God is absolutely holy in all His ways, it stands to
reason His resulting acts will be absolutely fair and just. In
other words, God's holiness necessitates His justice. And further, because He is a majestic God—that is, He is altogether
supreme and majestic in every way—His justice must be
majestic or supreme. Thus, God is always fair in all that He
does. He truly is a just God.

And when we say that God is just, we also mean He is
righteous, for justice and righteousness are almost identical in their original scriptural usage. A God who would act
in a state of fairness, or justice, would likewise be a God
who would conduct Himself absolutely righteously. To
praise God, then, is an invitation to stand amazed at His
justice.

The Purity of God's Justice

The Hebrew words that express God as being just and right, in fact, refer to "straightness and rightness when measured by the standard of perfection."[1]

The Bible says, "I will proclaim the name of the LORD; how glorious is our God! He is the Rock; his work is perfect. Everything he does is just and fair. He is a faithful God who does no wrong; how just and upright he is!" (Deut. 32:3–4).

In picturing the purity of God's justice, A. W. Tozer states, "Justice embodies the idea of moral equity. Iniquity is the exact opposite; it is *in*-equity, the absence of equality from human thoughts and acts. Judgment is the application of equity to moral situations and may be favorable or unfavorable according to whether the one under examination has been equitable or inequitable in heart and conduct."[2]

As with all of God's attributes, justice is not merely one part of God's nature or character, but it is a picture of all that He is. He is not only just or fair at specific times that seem to require His fairness, but rather the purity of His essence dictates that He exists in a state of justice. Tozer explains, "Justice, when used of God, is a name we give to the way God is, nothing more, and when God acts justly He is not doing so to conform to an independent criterion, but simply acting like Himself in a given situation. As gold is an element in itself and can never change nor compromise but is gold wherever it is found, so God is God, always, only, fully God, and can never be other than He is."[3] Praise God for the purity of His justice!

The Equity of God's Justice

To speak of God's righteousness—which, as we established, is a term interchangeable with His justice—we usually are referring to that attribute that God employs to justify the righteous and to exalt them to honor and glory.

Herman Bavinck writes, "Even in the law every judge and also every individual Israelite is warned not to wrest the justice due to the poor, not to slay the righteous, not to take a bribe, and not to oppress the sojourner, the widow, and the orphan, (Exod. 23:6–9). Righteousness (justice) consists especially in this: that persons are not respected in judgment; that the small and the great shall be heard alike; that the judges shall not be afraid of the face of man, for the judgment is God's (Deut. 1:16, 17; 16:19; Lev. 19:20)."[4]

God's justice, then, concerns God's fairness. John Bisagno explains, "When we speak of God as just, it is also another way of saying that God is fair. In His love, He is compassionate. In His holiness, He is set apart from mankind. In His sovereignty He is absolute ruler. But as just or righteous, God is also our example of justice and fairness."[5]

N. H. Smith provides further clarification, "'Righteousness' involves the establishment of equal rights for all, and to this extent 'justice' is a same equivalent. . . ."[6]

The Victory of God's Justice

Consider for a moment the victory of God's justice wrought on Calvary. The gifted Bible teacher Harry A. Ironside helps us understand this victory. According to Dr. Ironside, when God forgives through the risen, glorified Jesus, He not only forgives, but He justifies. It is impossible, Ironside explains, for an earthly judge to both forgive and justify a man. If a man is justified, he does not need to be forgiven.

Imagine a man charged with a crime going into a court, Ironside suggests, and, after the evidence is all in, he is pronounced not guilty and the judge sets him free. Then someone says, as he leaves the building, "I want to congratulate you. It was very kind of the judge to forgive you."

"Forgive? He did not forgive me; I was justified. There's nothing to forgive."

Ironside explains that you cannot justify a man if he does a wicked thing, but you can forgive him. God, however, not only forgives, but He justifies the ungodly, because He links the believer with Christ and makes him "accepted in the Beloved."

John Bisagno adds further insight into this beautiful attribute: "We can best understand the just nature of God by focusing our attention on His action of justification through Jesus Christ. Because God is just, He can bring us into a state of justification."[7] He adds, "Volumes could be written on the theological aspects of justification, but it is, simply stated, that I stand complete in Him, clothed in righteousness, accepted in the Beloved as though I had never been what I was before."[8]

Bisagno concludes, "When we stand before God in judgment, we stand condemned, unless we have faith in Jesus Christ. The key factor in God's judgment, then, is faith in Jesus Christ. If we have faith in Christ, God's just nature allows us to stand in a state of justification before Him (Acts 13:39)."[9]

There is, indeed, a sense of triumph in one's recognition of God's justice. Bavinck asserts, "God is perfect and righteous, and acts in accordance with justice. His righteousness consists especially in this: that He recognizes the justice of the righteous, and that He causes it to be brought to light and to triumph."[10]

God's justice encourages believers because He will never require that which they are unable to give. Bisagno relates, "Our God is generous as well as benevolent. He exhibits lovingkindness as well as understanding. He does not demand what we are incapable of giving, but instead He gives us what we are incapable of finding on our own."[11]

The Sovereignty of God's Justice

Because God is totally sovereign in all He does, He would naturally be sovereign in His administration of justice. In other words, God alone knows what is truly just or right for any given situation. Tozer reminds us of the Christian philosopher and saint Anselm, archbishop of Canterbury, who prayerfully sought a solution to what appeared to be a contradiction between God's justice and His mercy.

"How dost thou spare the wicked," Anselm inquired of God, "if thou art . . . supremely just?"

Anselm looked directly to God's nature and character for his answer, for he knew that it could be found only in *what* God *is*. Tozer continues, "Anselm's finding may be paraphrased this way: God's being is unitary; it is not composed of a number of parts working harmoniously, but simply one. There is nothing in His justice which forbids the exercise of His mercy."[12]

Anselm discovered that God's justice flows out of His sovereignty. He governs the universe as He pleases, for what He pleases is that which is best, and only God can know what is always truly best. Probing this study further, William B. Pope writes, "The legislative righteousness of God is the attribute that stamps perfectness on all the laws by which God carries on the government of the universe, whether in other worlds or in this; and whether His laws are revealed in the constitution of man's heart, or in the written revelation of His will. Scripture says, 'The LORD is our judge, the LORD is our lawgiver, the LORD is our king: he will save us' (Isa. 33:22)."[13]

The theologian continues, "We are required to believe that His Divine law is perfect: perfect as the expression of the Divine holiness; perfect therefore as the standard of right; perfect in its universal adaption; perfect in its requirements; perfect in its sanction. All this is summed into one sentence by St. Paul: 'The law is holy, and the commandment holy, and just, and good' (Rom. 7:12)."[14]

The Severity and Beauty of God's Justice

There are times that God's justice can appear, at a glance, to be a negative quality of His nature, especially when His justice requires His wrath. For example, God's justice requires the punishment of all evil. Further, God's justice actually required Jesus to become "the offering for our sin" (2 Cor. 5:21). This was necessary, to be sure, to obtain our very redemption.

Likewise, the Bible tells us that Jesus is the "sacrifice for our sins. He takes away not only our sins but the sins of all the world" (1 John 2:2). Think of it! God's justice required that a sinless, innocent man—God's incarnate Son—had to die so that we might be eternally free of the stain of sin. Christ's shed blood covers our sin and blots it out. Thus, when God looks at what was once our sin, He sees only the shed blood of His Son.

Consider also that God is just, or absolutely fair, in His pardon of sins, for salvation in Christ is available to *any* individual who chooses to accept it in faith. Paul reminded the Christians at Rome that they were "not guilty." Paul wrote: "Yet now God in his gracious kindness declares us not guilty. He has done this through Christ Jesus, who has freed us by taking away our sins. For God sent Jesus to take the punishment for our sins and to satisfy God's anger against us. We are made right with God when we believe that Jesus shed his blood, sacrificing his life for us . . ." (Rom. 3:24–25).

Finally, there are times that, in order for God to be fair, He must act in ways that appear to be unfair, even severe. But as the surgeon cuts out portions of the body infected by a cancer in order to save the whole, God's justice may necessitate apparently painful action. Perhaps in your own experience you can recall encountering a difficult situation during which you cried out to God, "That's just not fair," only to learn later how truly right God's actions were in that circumstance. Only then did you see that God selected that path for your own well-being.

In this sense, what appears at first glance to be a picture of severity becomes, in the end, a picture of beauty. Joseph, for example, was rejected by evil brothers and sold into slavery (Gen. 37:28). His brothers could not have known that God would turn this circumstance around for His glory and that Joseph would rise to prominence in Egypt, even to the point of Joseph being in a position to help sustain those very brothers through a devastating famine (Gen. 45:5–9).

Thank God for the totality of His infinite "fairness." The Bible says, ". . . Righteousness and justice are the foundation of his throne" (Ps. 97:2); and , ". . . Should not the Judge of all the earth do what is right?" (Gen. 18:25).

Beloved, *God is always fair!*

Sunday

Father God . . . You are—JUST!

JUST: Having a basis in or conforming to fact or reason. Morally and legally right; fair and reasonable; correct, proper and exacting.

Lord, You conform fully to that which is morally and legally right. Because You are just, You are exacting and proper in all Your ways. You are the God who is always fair. I rejoice in Your justice.
Your Word declares . . .

Your arm is endued with power; your hand is strong, your right hand exalted. Righteousness and justice are the foundation of your throne; love and faithfulness go before you.

Psalm 89:13–14 NIV

. . . He is clothed in dazzling splendor. We cannot imagine the power of the Almighty, yet he is so just and merciful . . .

Job 37:22–23

His ever expanding, peaceful government will never end. He will rule forever with fairness and justice from the throne of his ancestor David. The passionate commitment of the LORD Almighty will guarantee this!

Isaiah 9:7

Great are the works of the LORD; they are pondered by all who delight in them. . . . The works of his hands are faithful and just; all his precepts are trustworthy.

Psalm 111:2, 7 NIV

Lord . . . I Praise Your JUSTICE!

Monday

Father God . . . You are—INVINCIBLE!

INVINCIBLE: To exist in a state that is unconquerable and unpregnable; that which is impossible to overcome, penetrate or subdue; that which is beyond vulnerability.

Lord, You are invincible—the God beyond vulnerability. And because You surround me with Your presence, I cannot be conquered, overcome or subdued. You are my fortress of invincibility, my strong tower of defense.
Your Word declares . . .

Now to the King eternal, immortal, invisible, the only God, be honor and glory for ever and ever. Amen.

1 Timothy 1:17 NIV

Open up, ancient gates! Open up, ancient doors, and let the King of glory enter. Who is the King of glory? The LORD, strong and mighty, the LORD, invincible in battle.

Psalm 24:7–8

Sing a new song to the LORD! Sing his praises from the ends of the earth! . . . Let the coastlands glorify the LORD; let them sing his praise. The LORD will march forth like a mighty man; he will come out like a warrior, full of fury. He will shout his thundering battle cry, and he will crush all his enemies.

Isaiah 42:10, 12–13

O Sovereign LORD! You have made the heavens and earth by your great power. Nothing is too hard for you! You are loving and kind to thousands, though children suffer for their parents' sins. You are the great and powerful God, the LORD Almighty.

Jeremiah 32:17–18

Lord . . . I Praise Your INVINCIBILITY!

Tuesday

Father God . . . You are—BEAUTIFUL!

BEAUTIFUL: An appearance or perception that stirs a heightened response of the senses and of the mind at its highest level. To be full of a sense that arouses a strong contemplative delight. To be clothed in loveliness.

Lord, to look upon You is to gaze upon measureless beauty. You are loveliness at the highest level—the personification of absolute delight. To see Your glory is to see a glory human words cannot describe. You are, O Lord, infinitely beautiful.

Your Word declares . . .

One thing I ask of the LORD, this is what I seek: that I may dwell in the house of the LORD all the days of my life, to gaze upon the beauty of the LORD and to seek him in his temple.

Psalm 27:4 NIV

Great is the LORD! He is most worthy of praise! He is to be revered above all gods. . . . Honor and majesty surround him; strength and beauty are in his dwelling.

1 Chronicles 16:25, 27

In that day the Branch of the LORD will be beautiful and glorious, and the fruit of the land will be the pride and glory of the survivors in Israel. . . . Then the LORD will create over all of Mount Zion and over those who assemble there a cloud of smoke by day and a glow of flaming fire by night; over all the glory will be a canopy. It will be a shelter and shade from the heat of the day, and a refuge and hiding place from the storm and rain.

Isaiah 4:2, 5–6 NIV

Lord . . . I Praise Your BEAUTY!

Wednesday

Father God . . . You are—KIND!

KIND: To possess or manifest a sympathetic, forbearing or pleasant nature. That which is marked by a benevolent tenderness and is characterized by acts of consideration.

Lord, I pause to acknowledge the beauty of Your tenderness. Truly You are pleasant, sympathetic and forbearing; tender, considerate and understanding. I praise Your marvelous pleasantness.
Your Word declares . . .

The LORD is kind and merciful, slow to get angry, full of unfailing love. The LORD is good to everyone. He showers compassion on all his creation. All of your works will thank you, LORD, and your faithful followers will bless you.

Psalm 145:8–10

How kind the LORD is! How good he is! So merciful, this God of ours! The LORD protects those of childlike faith; I was facing death, and then he saved me.

Psalm 116:5–6

"For a brief moment I abandoned you, but with great compassion I will take you back. In a moment of anger I turned my face away for a little while. But with everlasting love I will have compassion on you," says the LORD, your Redeemer. . . . "For the mountains may depart and the hills disappear, but even then I will remain loyal to you. My covenant of blessing will never be broken," says the LORD, who has mercy on you.

Isaiah 54:7–8, 10

I will tell of the kindnesses of the LORD, the deeds for which he is to be praised, according to all the LORD has done for us—yes, the many good things he has done for the house of Israel, according to his compassion and many kindnesses.

Isaiah 63:7 NIV

Lord . . . I Praise Your KINDNESS!

Thursday

Father God . . . You are—RESPONSIVE!

RESPONSIVE: The quality or nature of reacting readily to suggestions, influences, appeals or efforts. A spirit of sensitivity manifested by positive and cooperative reactions.

Lord, I rejoice in spiritual praise for Your unfailing responsiveness to the urgency of my cries. You are not only present but present to react to my every need. I glory in the immediacy of Your ever-present availability.
Your Word declares . . .

This is what the LORD says, he who made the earth, the LORD who formed it and established it—the LORD is his name: "Call to me and I will answer you and tell you great and unsearchable things you do not know."

Jeremiah 33:2–3 NIV

Have mercy on me, O God, have mercy! I look to you for protection. I will hide beneath the shadow of your wings until this violent storm is past. I cry out to God Most High, to God who will fulfill his purpose for me. He will send help from heaven to save me, rescuing me from those who are out to get me. My God will send forth his unfailing love and faithfulness.

Psalm 57:1–3

Then when you call, the LORD will answer. "Yes, I am here," he will quickly reply. . . . The LORD will guide you continually, watering your life when you are dry and keeping you healthy, too. You will be like a well-watered garden, like an ever-flowing spring.

Isaiah 58:9a, 11

The LORD says, "I will rescue those who love me. I will protect those who trust in my name. When they call on me, I will answer; I will be with them in trouble. I will rescue them and honor them. I will satisfy them with a long life and give them my salvation."

Psalm 91:14–16

Lord . . . I Praise Your RESPONSIVENESS!

Friday

Father God . . . You are—CHANGELESS!

CHANGELESS: That which is incapable of alteration or change. To be fixed in character, nature and essence. The quality of being unaffected by external circumstances. To be consistent.

Lord, I glory in Your unchanging consistency and abound in Your absolute immutability. Although my emotions often dictate my reaction to circumstances, You are forever changeless, incapable of alteration.
Your Word declares . . .

. . . "The Lord is my helper, so I will not be afraid. What can mere mortals do to me?" . . . Jesus Christ is the same yesterday, today, and forever.

Hebrews 13:6, 8

In ages past you laid the foundation of the earth, and the heavens are the work of your hands. Even they will perish, but you remain forever; they will wear out like old clothing. You will change them like a garment, and they will fade away. But you are always the same; your years never end.

Psalm 102:25–27

In the beginning, O Lord, you laid the foundations of the earth, and the heavens are the work of your hands. They will perish, but you remain; they will all wear out like a garment. You will roll them up like a robe; like a garment they will be changed. But you remain the same, and your years will never end.

Hebrews 1:10–12 NIV

Lord . . . I Praise Your CHANGELESSNESS!

Saturday

Father God . . . You are—FORGIVING!

FORGIVING: The attitude and action of showing an inclination to pardon, absolve or grant relief from that which is required or something that is owed, especially when payment is not possible.

Lord, I abound in a recognition that You are the God who forgives. Because You are loving, You are forgiving. I accept Your forgiveness for all my sins and failures. I rejoice in the relief You have granted me through the shedding of Christ's blood on the cross.
Your Word declares . . .

The LORD is merciful and gracious; he is slow to get angry and full of unfailing love. He will not constantly accuse us, nor remain angry forever. He has not punished us for all our sins, nor does he deal with us as we deserve. For his unfailing love toward those who fear him is as great as the height of the heavens above the earth. He has removed our rebellious acts as far away from us as the east is from the west.

Psalm 103:8–12

Bring joy to your servant, for to you, O Lord, I lift up my soul. You are forgiving and good, O Lord, abounding in love to all who call to you.

Psalm 86:4–5 NIV

Seek the Lord while he may be found; call on him while he is near. Let the wicked forsake his way and the evil man his thoughts. Let him turn to the Lord, and he will have mercy on him, and to our God, for he will freely pardon.

Isaiah 55:6–7 NIV

Related references—Daniel 9:9; Nehemiah 9:17; Ephesians 4:32.

Lord . . . I Praise Your FORGIVENESS!

Summary of Week Four

Father God, You Are . . .
    JUST,
        INVINCIBLE,
            BEAUTIFUL
                and KIND;
    RESPONSIVE,
        CHANGELESS
            and FORGIVING!

Week Five

Amazed at God's Faithfulness

I will praise you forever, O God, for what you have done.

Psalm 52:9

It had become a simple habit. The night prior to leaving on any ministry-related trip I would go into the bedroom of my two daughters for special prayer. On this particular occasion it was the evening before I was to fly from California to Washington, D.C. I explained to Dena and Ginger the spiritual nature of the trip.

Resting motionless between the two girls, one arm wrapped tightly around each, I told them how much I loved them and needed their prayers.

"Pray for me, girls," I asked gently, immediately adding, "that God will be with me as I go to Washington."

I was startled by Dena's instant reply. Her words seemed almost shocking coming from a six-year-old child.

"That's really dumb, Daddy," she said firmly.

Quickly she added, "Why should we ask God to do something He's already promised He would do anyway!"

Chuckling at the thought of having a six-year-old "theologian" lying beside me, I couldn't help but recognize the reality of what I heard. God, indeed, could never be closer to us than He is right now. Further, His promises could *never* be more real. And because He is a God of absolutes, He will always be absolutely faithful. The Bible emphasizes: "Understand, therefore, that the Lord your God is indeed God. He is the faithful God . . ." (Deut. 7:9). Praise of our heavenly Father is to stand amazed at His faithfulness.

Arthur W. Pink comments, "This quality [faithfulness] is essential to His being, for without it He would not be God. For God to be unfaithful would be to act contrary to His nature, which would be impossible: 'If we believe not, yet he abideth faithful: he cannot deny himself' (2 Tim. 2:13)." Pink adds, "Faithfulness is one of the glorious perfections of God's being. He is as it were clothed with it: 'O Lord of hosts, who is a strong Lord like unto thee? Or to thy faithfulness round about thee?' (Ps. 89:9)."[1]

The Vastness of God's Faithfulness

There is, indeed, a vastness to God's faithfulness that many believers have not explored. The psalmist wrote, "Your unfailing love, O Lord, is as vast as the heavens; your faithfulness reaches beyond the clouds" (Ps. 36:5). Arthur Pink adds this commentary: "Far above all finite comprehension is the unchanging faithfulness of God. Everything about God is great, vast, incomparable. He never forgets, never fails, never falters, never forfeits His Word."[2]

Even in Jeremiah's deepest grief over the sins of God's people, he found the strength to cry out in defense of a God who, in actuality, needs no defending. Jeremiah wrote ". . . His compassions never fail. They are new every morning; great is your faithfulness" (Lam. 3:22–23 NIV).

The Completeness of God's Faithfulness

God's faithfulness is not only vast but vastly complete. It is all that it could possibly be. It cannot be improved on because it is faithfulness at its highest level of perfection. Discussing this quality of God's character, William B. Pope writes:

> Appeals to God's own faithfulness on the part of Jehovah, and responses to the appeal on the part of man, crowd the Scriptures. It may suffice here to refer to three most interesting illustrations of it in God's economy of grace. Sinners repenting of their sin, and confessing it are assured that "he is faithful and just to forgive us our sins" (1 John 1:9). Believers oppressed by the weariness of the way, and their own instability, are reminded that "The Lord is faithful, who shall stablish you, and keep you from evil" (2 Thess. 3:3). Finally, we are encouraged to aspire to perfect holiness of body and soul and spirit, and are assured that "Faithful is he that calleth you, who also will do it" (1 Thess. 5:24). These passages carry the Divine fidelity into the entire process of personal salvation from beginning to end.[3]

The Uniqueness of God's Faithfulness

Because God is holy as well as faithful, it stands to reason that His faithfulness will always be a holy faithfulness. Thus, there will be times that God's faithfulness will necessitate His faithfulness in areas that we might wish He would overlook.

For example, God must be faithful in disciplining His children. The psalmist said, "The suffering you sent was good for me, for it taught me to pay attention to your principles" (Ps. 119:71). A paraphrase of this verse reads, "The punishment you gave me was the best thing that could have happened to me, for it taught me to pay attention to your laws" (TLB). Earlier the psalmist said, "I used to wander off until you punished me; now I closely follow all you say" (Ps. 119:67 TLB).

Surely a faithful father cautiously guards his children from danger. But, there are certainly those occasions when all warnings go unheeded and discipline becomes necessary. Faithfulness requires it.

God's unique faithfulness also is seen when He chooses not to answer our prayers in ways we might anticipate. John Bisagno provides a powerful example. He had been away from his family for several weeks and longed to see them, even for one day. Because there was a two-day gap in his schedule, the minister decided to take the long flight home, departing as soon as he finished his last speaking engagement and returning two days later. Rushing to the airport, his heart was filled with a strange anxiety that he might miss his plane. It was almost a sense of panic. Hurrying through the airport terminal, he muttered both prayers and reassurances to himself about catching the plane. But, to his deep disappointment, as he arrived at the gate the plane was departing.

The minister was heartsick. What would he say to his dear family? It was, unfortunately, the last flight home that night, and the only flight that possibly could have fit his schedule. Now it would be many days before he would see his family. Deep in his heart he felt God let him down.

But the next morning a strange thing happened. As Bisagno went to breakfast, he purchased a newspaper and looked in horror at the headlines. The very airplane he had missed by minutes had collided with another over the Grand Canyon. It was one of the worst air disasters in history and all lives had been lost. The "no" God had said to the preacher's prayer had been a "yes" in disguise. God honored his faithfulness.[4]

The Awareness of God's Faithfulness

As our awareness of God's faithfulness increases, our recognition of His peace grows. The Bible says, "God is our refuge and strength, always ready to help in times of trouble. So we will not fear, even if earthquakes come and the mountains crumble into the sea" (Ps. 46:1–2).

When God expresses His faithfulness in Scripture, He is simply declaring that He will always honor the promises of His Word. And because of that particular quality of God—His immutability—He cannot *and* will not change. Through our trials or struggles, He will ever be with us. No day will be too dark and no night too long that God will not faithfully carry us through.

During the German blitz on London during World War II, an elderly lady refused to move from the upstairs room at the front of her home. Her friends, deeply concerned for her safety, recommended she move to a safer place. Politely declining the suggestion, the woman confidently declared, "I says my prayers to God every night and I goes to sleep. There's no need for us both to keep awake."

Glory to God, He is ever awake, and He is ever faithful to His promises. The psalmist cried, ". . . we went through fire and water, but you brought us to a place of abundance" (Ps. 66:12 NIV). Annie Johnson Flint adds poetically:

> When thou passeth through the waters
>   Deep the waves may be and cold,
> But Jehovah is our refuge
>   And His promise is our hold;
> For the Lord Himself hath said it,
>   He, the faithful God and true—
> When thou comest through the waters
>   Thou shalt not go down but through.

The "Enoughness" of God's Faithfulness

To a degree God's righteousness and faithfulness form a bond that holds together all aspects of His nature and character. The prophet Isaiah wrote, "He will be clothed with fairness and truth" (Isa. 11:5). Praise the Lord—God's faithfulness will never fail. He is girded with a faithful dependability.

Years ago Pastor R. I. Williams telephoned his sermon topic to the *Northfolk Ledger Dispatch*. "The Lord Is My Shepherd," he told the editor. "Is that all?" he was asked. With a chuckle, the pastor replied, "That's enough!"

That week the church page announced Williams's sermon topic: "The Lord Is My Shepherd—That's Enough!" An apparent mistake contained a monumental truth. The Lord *is* my shepherd, and that *is* enough. And although I know of no dictionary that includes a listing of a word called "enoughness," such a word is worthy of implementation here. The definition might read something like this, "The state or quality of that which exists at a level of always being enough."

Beloved reader, God's faithfulness truly abounds in enoughness! Wise is that motto that for centuries has endured—JESUS NEVER FAILS!

Sunday

Father God . . . You are—FAITHFUL!

FAITHFUL: Adhering strictly to the person, cause or idea to which one is bound. Worthy of trust or credence. Consistently reliable, devoted and true. Unchanging in attachment toward the object to which one is committed.

Lord, with my lips I honor Your faithfulness. You are worthy of trust and credence, for You alone are consistently reliable in all that You do. I rejoice in Your unchanging commitment toward me, the object of Your love. You are my altogether faithful God!

Your Word declares . . .

Yet this I call to mind and therefore I have hope: Because of the LORD's great love we are not consumed, for his compassions never fail. They are new every morning; great is your faithfulness. I say to myself, "The LORD is my portion; therefore I will wait for him."

Lamentations 3:21–24 NIV

Understand, therefore, that the LORD your God is indeed God. He is the faithful God who keeps his covenant for a thousand generations and constantly loves those who love him and obey his commands.

Deuteronomy 7:9

Forever, O LORD, your word stands firm in heaven. Your faithfulness extends to every generation, as enduring as the earth you created.

Psalm 119:89–90

The highest angelic powers stand in awe of God. He is far more awesome than those who surround his throne. O LORD God Almighty! Where is there anyone as mighty as you, LORD? Faithfulness is your very character.

Psalm 89:7–8

Therefore you do not lack any spiritual gift as you eagerly wait for our Lord Jesus Christ to be revealed. He will keep you strong to the end, so that you will be blameless on the day of our Lord Jesus Christ. God, who has called you into fellowship with his Son Jesus Christ our Lord, is faithful.

1 Corinthians 1:7–9 NIV

Related references—1 Corinthians 10:13; 1 Thessalonians 5:23–24; Psalm 89:1–2.

Lord . . . I Praise Your FAITHFULNESS!

Monday

Father God . . . You are—POWERFUL!

POWERFUL: To be filled with the ability or capacity to act or perform any function effectively; that which is full of forceful effectiveness. Having all the energy needed to produce a desired effect; to possess absolute control or physical might.

Lord, I praise the fullness of Your universal power. All that You are is saturated with eternal energy and forceful effectiveness. Nothing is too hard for You. You are supreme in Your authority and absolute in Your ability. Glory, glory to Your inexhaustible might!
Your Word declares . . .

How great is our Lord! His power is absolute! His understanding is beyond comprehension! The LORD supports the humble, but he brings the wicked down into the dust.

Psalm 147:5–6

God has spoken plainly, and I have heard it many times: Power, O God, belongs to you.

Psalm 62:11

O God, you are my God; I earnestly search for you. My soul thirsts for you; my whole body longs for you in this parched and weary land where there is no water. I have seen you in your sanctuary and gazed upon your power and glory.

Psalm 63:1–2

He gives power to those who are tired and worn out; he offers strength to the weak. Even youths will become exhausted, and young men will give up. But those who wait on the Lord will find new strength. They will fly high on wings like eagles. They will run and not grow weary. They will walk and not faint.

Isaiah 40:29–31

Lord . . . I Praise Your POWER!

Tuesday

Father God . . . You are—HEALTHFUL!

HEALTH: That which is characterized by sound physical and mental well-being. To possess physical capacities that function optimally; to be wholesome, energetic and fit.

Lord, You are all that characterizes health and well-being. Only in You do I find true wholeness, fitness and physical energy. I rejoice in Your capacity to nurture and sustain. You are my restoration; You are my health! Praise the Lord!
Your Word declares . . .

"But all who devour you will be devoured; all your enemies will go into exile. Those who plunder you will be plundered; all who make spoil of you I will despoil. But I will restore you to health and heal your wounds," declares the LORD.

Jeremiah 30:16–17 NIV

Praise the LORD, I tell myself; with my whole heart, I will praise his holy name. Praise the LORD, I tell myself, and never forget the good things he does for me. He forgives all my sins and heals all my diseases. He ransoms me from death and surrounds me with love and tender mercies.

Psalm 103:1–4

"But for you who fear my name, the Sun of Righteousness will rise with healing in his wings. And you will go free, leaping with joy like calves let out to pasture. On the day when I act, you will tread upon the wicked as if they were dust under your feet," says the LORD Almighty.

Malachi 4:2–3

Praise the LORD! How good it is to sing praises to our God! How delightful and how right! The LORD is rebuilding Jerusalem and bringing the exiles back to Israel. He heals the brokenhearted, binding up their wounds.

Psalm 147:1–3

O LORD my God, I cried out to you for help, and you restored my health. You brought me up from the grave, O LORD. You kept me from falling into the pit of death. Sing to the LORD, all you godly ones! Praise his holy name.

Psalm 30:2–4

Related references—Exodus 15:26; Ezekiel 34:16.
Lord . . . I Praise Your HEALTHFULNESS!

Wednesday

Father God . . . You are—SECURE!

SECURE: Free from danger or risk of loss. Freedom from fear, doubt or worry. Not likely to fail or give way. That which provides shelter or refuge. The provision of safety and certainty.

Lord, I glory in the reality of Your security. Through Your power I am free from fear of any future loss. I find shelter in the certainty of Your presence and refuge in the reality of Your Word.

Your Word declares . . .

There is no one like the God of Israel. He rides across the heavens to help you, across the skies in majestic splendor. The eternal God is your refuge, and his everlasting arms are under you. He thrusts out the enemy before you; it is he who cries, "Destroy them!"

Deuteronomy 33:26–27

Lord, sustain me as you promised, that I may live! Do not let my hope be crushed. Sustain me, and I will be saved; then I will meditate on your principles continually.

Psalm 119:116–17

Many people say, "Who will show us better times?" Let the smile of your face shine on us, Lord. You have given me greater joy than those who have abundant harvests of grain and wine. I will lie down in peace and sleep, for you alone, O LORD, will keep me safe.

Psalm 4:6–8

My sheep recognize my voice; I know them, and they follow me.

I give them eternal life, and they will never perish. No one will snatch them away from me, for my Father has given them to me, and he is more powerful than anyone else. So no one can take them from me.

John 10:27–29

Related references—Job 11:18–19; Proverbs 18:10; Isaiah 25:4.

Lord . . . I Praise Your SECURITY!

Thursday

Father God . . . You are—PEACEFUL!

PEACE: Inner contentment and freedom from disturbing thoughts or emotional reactions. A state of calm, quiet and serenity. That which possesses order and unity.

Lord, You are the totality of all true contentment, the essence of calm serenity. In Your presence I find peace and freedom, for You alone exist in ordered unity.
Your Word declares . . .

Don't worry about anything; instead, pray about everything. Tell God what you need, and thank him for all he has done. If you do this, you will experience God's peace, which is far more wonderful than the human mind can understand. His peace will guard your hearts and minds as you live in Christ Jesus.

Philippians 4:6–7

But now in Christ Jesus you who once were far away have been brought near through the blood of Christ.
For he himself is our peace, who has made the two one and has destroyed the barrier, the dividing wall of hostility.

Ephesians 2:13–14 NIV

Peace I leave with you; my peace I give you. I do not give to you as the world gives. Do not let your hearts be troubled and do not be afraid.

John 14:27 NIV

You will keep in perfect peace all who trust in you, whose thoughts are fixed on you! Trust in the LORD always, for the LORD GOD is the eternal Rock.

Isaiah 26:3–4

The LORD gives his people strength. The LORD blesses them with peace.

Psalm 29:11

Lord . . . I Praise Your PEACE!

Friday

Father God . . . You are—RADIANT!

RADIANT: Filled with light; to glow and beam with brightness. That which is brilliant, luminous and lustrous.

Lord, with joy I gaze upon the glory of Your glowing essence. You shine with the brilliance of a lustrous purity and light the way to everything holy. Your every attribute abounds with brightness, for all that You are is clothed with heavenly radiance.
Your Word declares . . .

I prayed to the LORD, and he answered me, freeing me from all my fears. Those who look to him for help will be radiant with joy; no shadow of shame will darken their faces. I cried out to the LORD in my suffering, and he heard me. He set me free from all my fears.

Psalm 34:4–6

Please listen, O Shepherd of Israel, you who lead Israel like a flock. O God, enthroned above the cherubim, display your radiant glory to Ephraim, Benjamin, and Manasseh. Show us your mighty power. Come to rescue us! Turn us again to yourself, O God. Make your face shine down upon us. Only then will we be saved.

Psalm 80:1–3

The commandments of the Lᴏʀᴅ are right, bringing joy to the heart. The commands of the Lᴏʀᴅ are clear, giving insight to life. Reverence for the Lᴏʀᴅ is pure, lasting forever. The laws of the Lᴏʀᴅ are true; each one is fair. They are more desirable than gold, even the finest gold. They are sweeter than honey, even honey dripping from the comb.

Psalm 19:8–10

Arise, shine, for your light has come, and the glory of the Lᴏʀᴅ rises upon you. See, darkness covers the earth and thick darkness is over the peoples, but the Lᴏʀᴅ rises upon you and his glory appears over you. . . . Then you will look and be radiant, your heart will throb and swell with joy; the wealth on the seas will be brought to you, to you the riches of the nations will come.

Isaiah 60:1–2, 5 ɴɪᴠ

Lord . . . I Praise Your RADIANCE!

Saturday

Father God . . . You are—RIGHTEOUS!

RIGHTEOUS: Meeting the standards of that which is just and right. The quality of acting or being in accordance with what is honorable, right and free from guilt or wrong. To conduct oneself with moral and ethical excellence.

Lord, with this sacrifice of praise I declare Your righteousness. You are virtuous, noble, ethical and right. You more than meet any standards of moral excellence, for You are that standard—the very fountainhead of absolute rightness. I honor You, my honorable King!
Your Word declares . . .

"For the time is coming" says the LORD, "when I will place a righteous Branch on King David's throne. He will be a King who rules with wisdom. He will do what is just and right throughout the land. And this is his name: 'The LORD Is Our Righteousness.' In that day Judah will be saved, and Israel will live in safety."

Jeremiah 23:5–6

Your unfailing love, O LORD, is as vast as the heavens; your faithfulness reaches beyond the clouds. Your righteousness is like the mighty mountains, your justice like the ocean depths. You care for people and animals alike, O LORD.

Psalm 36:5–6

Your throne is founded on two strong pillars—righteousness and justice. Unfailing love and truth walk before you as attendants. Happy are those who hear the joyful call to worship, for they will walk in the light of your presence, LORD. They rejoice all day long in your wonderful reputation. They exult in your righteousness.

Psalm 89:14–16

How amazing are the deeds of the LORD! All who delight in him should ponder them. Everything he does reveals his glory and majesty. His righteousness never fails. Who can forget the wonders he performs? How gracious and merciful is our LORD!

Psalm 111:2–4

Lord . . . I Praise Your RIGHTEOUSNESS!

Summary of Week Five

Father God, You Are . . .
> FAITHFUL,
>> POWERFUL,
>>> HEALTHFUL
>>>> and SECURE;
> PEACEFUL,
>> RADIANT
>>> and RIGHTEOUS!

Week Six

Amazed at God's Mercy

How kind the LORD is! How good he is! So merciful, this
God of ours!

Psalm 116:5

~✺~

Sadly, there are some aspects of God's nature described so
often that the fullness of their meaning almost eludes us.
Consider the word "merciful." It contains an unusually
significant depth of meaning. Mercy is defined as "the giving of a second chance." Full means "having in it all there
is space for." The combination of these two words to form
"merciful"—when applied to an infinite, eternal Being we
call God—is infinitely significant. It denotes God being
full of, or containing, all the possible second chances any
of us could ever need. Because all His attributes are inexhaustible, His supply of second chances is inexhaustible.
Thus, to praise God for who He is, is to stand amazed at
His unbounding mercy.

146

Naturally, a close relationship between God's attributes of love and mercy can be noted, and one might even be inclined to view them as one. They are, however, distinct. John Bisagno points out that the dictionary defines love as "an affection based on admiration or benevolence"; and "warm attraction." Mercy, on the other hand, is "a compassion or forbearance shown to an offender or subject." It also is defined as "a blessing that is an act of divine favor or compassion."

The author concludes that "love, then, is that feeling God has toward us, whom He has created. Mercy, on the other hand, is an attitude He takes toward us who are not worthy of His pardon."[1] Arthur W. Pink explains, "God's mercy denotes His ready inclination to relieve the misery of fallen creatures. Thus, God's mercy presupposes sin."[2]

The Gift of God's Mercy

It is difficult to define the word mercy without using words like "love" and "grace." Specifically addressing the theme of "grace," William B. Pope states, "This word (grace) is in some respects a creation of the gospel. God was, in the Old Testament, a 'God full of compassion, and gracious, longsuffering, and plenteous in mercy and truth' (Ps. 86:15); but there is something in this Evangelical term that surpasses all these. In the New Testament this unwearied agent of love appears as the 'Grace of the Lord Jesus Christ,' which is only another form of the 'love of God' and this again only another form of the 'communion of the Holy Ghost' (2 Cor. 13:14)."[3]

Mercy, then, is a direct outflow of God's love as is His grace. In defining mercy Bisagno writes, "'To relieve the miseries' may be the best way to state that characteristic of God which causes Him to extend mercy on our behalf."

Bisagno continues, "In the Old Testament, the point at which God expressed His love in the forgiveness of sin was at a place called 'the mercy seat.' Here the high priest annually placed the blood of a sacrificial lamb so that the Holy God might show mercy to His sinning people. It is at the point of condescending mercy that God has fellowship with people."[4] The author concludes, "God does not have to accept sinful people. God's perfection could cause Him to shun His imperfect creatures. But because of His mercy, God literally reaches down and touches us who do not deserve such treatment from the Holy Being."[5]

Such is the mercy of God. It is love and grace combined. It is God expressing His love in unqualified forgiveness. It is God's gift of second chances. It is that quality of God's essence that causes us to shout in agreement with Joseph Addison,

> With all thy mercies, O my God
> My rising soul surveys,
> Transported with the view, I'm lost
> In wonder, love, and praise.[6]

The Abundance of God's Mercy

God's mercy is not merely a single facet of His nature but a quality of His entire being. Because any quality that God is, He is completely, we must declare Him to be absolutely and fully forgiving. His mercy is abundant beyond any capacity to deplete it. Pink says, "When we contemplate the characteristics of His divine excellency, we cannot do otherwise than bless God for it. His mercy is 'great' (1 Kings 3:6), 'plenteous' (Ps. 86:5), 'tender' (Luke 1:78), 'abundant' (1 Peter 1:3). It is 'from everlasting to everlasting upon them that fear him' (Ps. 103:17). Well may we say with the Psalmist, 'I will sing aloud of thy mercy' (Ps. 59:16)."[7]

Revival preacher Leonard Ravenhill told of a humorous experience that occurred years ago as he walked by a Sunday school classroom filled with little children, five or six years of age. They were sitting on chairs of such a height that their feet dangled above the floor. Just as the preacher passed, they began to sing the words of the much-loved hymn, "Years I spent in vanity and pride!"

Although I, too, chuckled at the thought of five-year-old children singing of spending years in vanity and pride, there is a powerful truth in those endearing words. Look again at the chorus of William Newell's hymn:

> Mercy there was great, and grace was free;
> Pardon there was multiplied to me.
> There my burdened soul found liberty,
> At Calvary.

God's mercy is truly great. The Bible says, "For Your mercy reaches unto the heavens" (Ps. 57:10 NKJV), to which Arthur W. Pink adds, "The riches of God's mercy transcend our loftiest thought. 'For as the heaven is high above the earth, so great is his mercy toward them that fear him' (Ps. 103:11). None can measure it. The elect are designated 'vessels of mercy' (Rom. 9:23). It is mercy that quickened them when they were dead in sin (Eph. 2:4, 5). It is mercy that saves them (Titus 3:5). It is His abundant mercy which begat them unto an eternal inheritance (1 Peter 1:3). Time would fail us to tell of His preserving, sustaining, pardoning, supplying mercy. Unto His own, God is 'the Father of mercies' (2 Cor. 1:3)."[8]

Thomas Moore said it especially well in the last line of his beautiful hymn, "Come Ye Disconsolate":

> Come, ye disconsolate, where-e'er ye languish,
>   Come to the mercy seat, fervently kneel;
> Here bring your wounded hearts, here tell your anguish;
>   Earth has no sorrow that heaven cannot heal.[9]

The Nature of God's Mercy

A. W. Tozer provides this meaningful overview of the nature of God's mercy: "Mercy is an attribute of God, an infinite and inexhaustible energy within the divine nature which disposes God to be actively compassionate."[10]

He explains, "Were there no guilt in the world, no pain and no tears, God would yet be infinitely merciful; but His mercy might well remain hidden in His heart, unknown to the created universe."[11]

Nothing can prevent God from being merciful because it is His very nature. He was, in fact, a God of mercy before man ever came on the scene. In other words, that quality of His nature from which His second chances would someday flow has always and infinitely existed. Look again to the thoughts of Tozer, "Mercy never began to be, but from eternity was; so it will never cease to be. Nothing that has occurred will occur in heaven or earth or hell that can change the tender mercies of our God. Forever His mercy stands, a boundless, overwhelming immensity of divine pity and compassion."[12]

This, of course, is not to say that God will ever compromise His justice or holiness because of His mercy. Pink declares, "What a mercy that in the New Jerusalem 'there shall in no wise enter into it any thing that defileth, neither whatsoever worketh abomination' (Rev. 21:27)!"

Probing this thought further, Pink explains, "Lest the reader might think in the last paragraph we have been drawing upon our imagination, let us appeal to Holy Scripture in support of what has been said. In Psalm 143:12 we find David praying, 'And of thy mercy cut off mine enemies, and destroy all them that afflict my soul: for I am thy servant.' Again, in Psalm 136:15 we read that God 'overthrew Pharoah and his host in the Red Sea: for his mercy endureth for ever.' It was an act of vengeance upon

Pharoah and his hosts, but it was an act of 'mercy' upon the Israelites."[13]

The Beauty of God's Mercy

A friend once showed the gifted artist John Ruskin an expensive handkerchief on which a blot of ink had left an ugly mark.

"Nothing can be done with this now," said the friend, crumbling the handkerchief and preparing to discard it.

Although it was an unusual request, the artist asked if he could keep the handkerchief. After a time he returned it to his friend, who was absolutely amazed at what he saw. With India ink the artist had made a unique design using the ugly blot as the focus of his creation. What had once appeared worthless was now a treasured work of beauty.

So it is with the mercy of God. What once was marred by sin and spiritual decay now shines with the beauty of God's mercy. And, most exciting, His mercy holds for us eternal ramifications. Through God's mercy we have eternal life in addition to the security of knowing that our failures cannot exceed God's capacity to forgive. Praise God for the power of His measureless mercy. Tozer declares, "When through the blood of the everlasting covenant we children of the shadows reach at last our home in the light, we shall have a thousand strings to our harps, but the sweetest may well be the one tuned to sound forth most perfectly the mercy of God."[14]

Sunday

Father God . . . You are—MERCIFUL!

MERCIFUL: To be full of compassion and leniency; to manifest an unusually benevolent spirit of forgiveness; to show unusual compassion, leniency or tolerance to victims of misfortune.

Lord, joyfully my words of praise rise heavenward in honor of Your mercy. You are truly full of second chances for Your children. I rejoice in Your abundant forgiveness and praise Your compassionate leniency. Glory to Your unsearchable benevolence.
Your Word declares . . .

How amazing are the deeds of the LORD! All who delight in him should ponder them. Everything he does reveals his glory and majesty. His righteousness never fails. Who can forget the wonders he performs? How gracious and merciful is our LORD!

Psalm 111:2–4

But you, O Lord, are a merciful and gracious God, slow to get angry, full of unfailing love and truth.

Psalm 86:15

From there you will search again for the Lord your God. And if you search for him with all your heart and soul, you will find him. . . . For the Lord your God is merciful—he will not abandon you or destroy you or forget the solemn covenant he made with your ancestors.

Deuteronomy 4:29, 31

How kind the Lord is! How good he is! So merciful, this God of ours! The Lord protects those of childlike faith; I was facing death, and then he saved me.

Psalm 116:5–6

Lord . . . I Praise Your MERCY!

Monday

Father God . . . You are—JOYFUL!

JOY: A condition or feeling of bliss, delight, enjoyment and pleasure; gratification, jubilation or celebration. The state of happiness or gladness.

Lord, You are truly my joy. Your presence brings me gratification, enjoyment and bliss. In You I find pleasure in its purest form and a revelation of infinite happiness. You are my gladness and delight.
Your Word declares . . .

You will go out in joy and be led forth in peace; the mountains and hills will burst into song before you, and all the trees of the field will clap their hands.

Isaiah 55:12 NIV

. . . This day is sacred to our Lord. Do not grieve, for the joy of the LORD is your strength.

Nehemiah 8:10 NIV

When you obey me, you remain in my love, just as I obey my Father and remain in his love. I have told you this so that you will be filled with my joy. Yes, your joy will overflow!

John 15:10–11

Sing to the Lord, all you godly ones! Praise his holy name. His anger lasts for a moment, but his favor lasts a lifetime! Weeping may go on all night, but joy comes with the morning.

Psalm 30:4–5

Lord . . . I Praise Your JOYFULNESS!

Tuesday

Father God . . . You are—INFINITE!

INFINITE: Greater than any preassigned finite value however large. Immeasurable or unaccountably large. Unlimited in special extent. Continuing endlessly in time. Boundless, vast, immense and inexhaustible. That which extends to infinity. Unconfined and immense.

Lord, who could possibly fix a measure on Your boundlessness. You are greater in worth than any preassigned finite value and immeasurable by any standard of evaluation. You are unlimited in special extent and inexhaustible in marvelous glory. I praise Your unconfined infinity.

Your Word declares . . .

Lord, through all the generations you have been our home! Before the mountains were created, before you made the earth and the world, you are God, without beginning or end. . . . For you, a thousand years are as yesterday! They are like a few hours!

Psalm 90:1–2, 4

The LORD builds up Jerusalem; He gathers together the outcasts of Israel. He heals the brokenhearted and binds up their wounds. He counts the number of the stars; He calls them all by name. Great is our Lord, and mighty in power; His understanding is infinite.

Psalm 147:2–5 NKJV

I know that you are pleased with me, for my enemy does not triumph over me. In my integrity you uphold me and set me in your presence forever. Praise be to the LORD, the God of Israel, from everlasting to everlasting. Amen and Amen.

Psalm 41:11–13 NIV

Lord . . . I Praise Your INFINITY!

Wednesday

Father God . . . You are—STABLE!

STABLE: Immutable and permanent. The quality of being steady in purpose; constant, durable and enduring. To be mentally well-balanced. To be resistant to sudden change of position or condition.

Lord, Your essence is that of absolute consistency. You are immutable and enduring. I rejoice in the recognition that You are resistant to all change and completely stable in Your nature and character. I praise Your steadfast durability.
Your Word declares . . .

I wait quietly before God, for my hope is in him. He alone is my rock and my salvation, my fortress where I will not be shaken. My salvation and my honor come from God alone. He is my refuge, a rock where no enemy can reach me.

Psalm 62:5–7

The LORD is my rock, my fortress, and my savior; my God is my rock, in whom I find protection. He is my shield, the strength of my salvation, and my stronghold. . . . The LORD lives! Blessed be my rock! May the God of my salvation be exalted!

Psalm 18:2, 46

Bend down and listen to me; rescue me quickly. Be for me a great rock of safety, a fortress where my enemies cannot reach me. You are my rock and my fortress. For the honor of your name, lead me out of this peril.

Psalm 31:2–3

Though the LORD is very great and lives in heaven, he will make Jerusalem his home of justice and righteousness. In that day he will be your sure foundation, providing a rich store of salvation, wisdom, and knowledge. The fear of the LORD is the key to this treasure.

Isaiah 33:5–6

Lord . . . I Praise Your STABILITY!

Thursday

Father God . . . You are—WONDERFUL!

WONDERFUL: That which is filled with the capacity to excite astonishment, surprise and delight. To cause a sense of marvel, admiration or awe.

Lord, You are gloriously full of all that causes wonder. Your presence excites within me both astonishment and delight. You created all the extraordinary wonders of the universe and You are the greatest wonder of them all. I honor You, my wonderful Lord!

Your Word declares . . .

For a child is born to us, a son is given to us. And the government will rest on his shoulders. These will be his royal titles: Wonderful Counselor . . . His ever expanding, peaceful government will never end. He will rule forever with fairness and justice from the throne of his ancestor David. . . .

Isaiah 9:6–7

I see God, the Holy One, moving across the deserts from Edom and Mount Paran. His brilliant splendor fills the heavens, and the earth is filled with his praise! What a wonderful God he is! Rays of brilliant light flash from his hands. He rejoices in his awesome power.

Habakkuk 3:3–4

I am praying to you because I know you will answer, O God. Bend down and listen as I pray. Show me your unfailing love in wonderful ways. You save with your strength those who seek refuge from their enemies.

Psalm 17:6–7

Sing to him; yes, sing his praises. Tell everyone about his miracles. Exult in his holy name; O worshipers of the LORD, rejoice! Search for the LORD and for his strength, and keep on searching. Think of the wonderful works he has done, the miracles, and the judgments he handed down.

1 Chronicles 16:9–12

Oh, the joys of those who trust the LORD, who have no confidence in the proud, or in those who worship idols. O LORD my God, you have done many miracles for us. Your plans for us are too numerous to list. If I tried to recite all your wonderful deeds, I would never come to the end of them.

Psalm 40:4–5

But be sure to fear the LORD and sincerely worship him. Think of all the wonderful things he has done for you.

1 Samuel 12:24

Lord . . . I Praise Your WONDER!

Friday

Father God . . . You are—ACCESSIBLE!

ACCESSIBLE: The quality or nature of that which is easy to approach or enter. To be approachable and attainable. To readily permit admittance.

Lord, I glory in the awareness that You are infinitely accessible. Your nature is that of openness and ready admittance to all who would seek You with a pure heart. Thank You, Lord, for Your compassionate approachability.
Your Word declares . . .

Therefore, since we have been justified through faith, we have peace with God through our Lord Jesus Christ, through whom we have gained access by faith into this grace in which we now stand. And we rejoice in the hope of the glory of God.

Romans 5:1–2 NIV

[Christ] came and preached peace to you who were far away and peace to those who were near. For through him we both have access to the Father by one Spirit.

Ephesians 2:17–18 NIV

And so, dear friends, we can boldly enter heaven's Most Holy Place because of the blood of Jesus. This is the new, lifegiving way that Christ has opened up for us through the sacred curtain, by means of his death for us.

Hebrews 10:19–20

Come to me, all of you who are weary and carry heavy burdens, and I will give you rest. Take my yoke upon you. Let me teach you, because I am humble and gentle, and you will find rest for your souls. For my yoke fits perfectly, and the burden I give you is light.

Matthew 11:28–30

Lord . . . I Praise Your ACCESSIBILITY!

Saturday

Father God . . . You are—SOVEREIGN!

SOVEREIGN: That which governs from a position of superlative strength or efficiency. Supreme, unmitigated and unattested in authority. To rule in complete independence.

Lord, You are absolutely sovereign over Your universal kingdom. You alone reign in unmitigated and unattested authority. I fear no enemy, for all that exists in the universe must submit to Your authority. Glory to Your sovereign rulership.

Your Word declares . . .

Praise the name of God forever and ever, for he alone has all wisdom and power. He determines the course of world events; he removes kings and sets others on the throne. He gives wisdom to the wise and knowledge to the scholars. He reveals deep and mysterious things and knows what lies hidden in darkness, though he himself is surrounded by light.

Daniel 2:20–22

The Lord has made the heavens his throne; from there he rules over everything. Praise the Lord, you angels of his, you mighty creatures who carry out his plans, listening for each of his commands. Yes, praise the Lord, you armies of angels who serve him and do his will! Praise the Lord, everything he has created, everywhere in his kingdom. As for me—I, too, will praise the Lord.

Psalm 103:19–22

"Don't lift your fists in defiance at the heavens or speak with rebellious arrogance." For no one on earth—from east or west, or even from the wilderness—can raise another person up. It is God alone who judges; he decides who will rise and who will fall.

Psalm 75:5–7

Lord . . . I Praise Your SOVEREIGNTY!

Summary of Week Six

Father God, You Are . . .
    MERCIFUL,
        JOYFUL,
            INFINITE
                and STABLE;
    WONDERFUL,
        ACCESSIBLE
            and SOVEREIGN!

Week Seven

Amazed at God's Integrity

Send out your light and your truth; let them guide me. Let them lead me to your holy mountain, to the place where you live.

Psalm 43:3

"As to God's nature, His triune essence, His attributes or relations to Him and His to us, and all that concerns the essentials of our theology, we are absolutely dependent on the truth of the Creator."[1]

With this important comment from William B. Pope to inspire our thinking, let us examine that quality of God's character termed His integrity.

Without the integrity of God, everything He says about Himself in His Word would be open to question. Indeed, our list of ways to praise Him would be questionable. Because God's Word pictures Him as absolutely good— that is, the essence of all true goodness—we know that any quality or expression that describes that which is good can be used to describe God. Further, we can trust this to be true, precisely because of the integrity of God. Our daily praise thus becomes an open invitation to stand amazed at God's infinite integrity.

Each of us has faced the sad experience of discovering that someone failed us in his or her word. But the saddest consequence of such a discovery is not in the tragedy of a single act of betrayal but in the lack of trust it breeds in the relationship. From that point the person's veracity is questioned. Every act is suspect; every word comes under question.

This is why we rejoice in the recognition of the totality of God's integrity. He cannot lie. The Bible says, "God is not a man, that he should lie, nor a son of man, that he should change his mind. Does he speak and then not act? Does he promise and not fulfill?" (Num. 23:19 NIV).

The prophet Isaiah adds, "Search from the book of the LORD, and read: Not one of these shall fail; not one shall lack her mate. For My mouth has commanded it, and His Spirit has gathered them" (Isa. 34:16 NKJV).

The Meaning of God's Integrity

Truth, simply stated, is a declaration of something that is absolutely right in accordance with all the facts. Herman Bavinck explains, "When we ascribe metaphysical 'truth' to an object or a person, we mean that that object or person is all that it is supposed to be. In that sense, gold which is gold not only in appearance but in reality, is real, pure, 'true' gold."[2]

The totality of God's truth is especially revealed in His Son Jesus. Even Jesus declared Himself to be "the way, the truth, and the life" (John 14:6). Pope explains, "The Bible says God 'is the true God,' and 'the only true God' (1 John 5:20; John 17:3). It is observable that in both these passages, which are unique, the revelation of God is connected with the Son."[3]

Thus, when we read that Jesus Christ is "the truth," it means that His person is the embodiment of all perfection in accordance with what is absolutely right. *His essence is truth.* To touch Jesus is to touch "truth." To believe in Jesus is to believe in "truth." To accept Jesus into one's life is to accept the totality of truth into one's being.

Jesus Christ, indeed, is truth defined! "And you will know the truth, and the truth will set you free" (John 8:32).

The Essence of God's Integrity

A person is honest because the things he says and does measure up to standards that we (or society) have set as being right. God, however, is honest not because His acts are in accordance with some established criteria but because His essence is absolute truth. God is, quite simply, the personification of integrity. Herman Bavinck explains, "God is the truth in all its absolute fullness. Hence, He is the 'original truth,' the source of all truth, the truth of all truth, the ground of all truth, and all the true essence of all things, of their knowability and conceivability; the ideal and archetype of all truth, of all ethical reality, and of all laws and regulations."[4]

And because God exists in absolute truth, His written communication to man must be absolutely true. Bavinck further explains, "God's revelation corresponds exactly to His being . . . our conceptions are true if they are an exact copy of reality. Taken in this sense, 'truth' is opposed to 'error.'"[5]

The Scope of God's Integrity

Consider, too, the vast scope of God's integrity. Pope suggests, "Truth as a Divine perfection represents the absolute correspondence of all God's revelations with reality; and it may be referred to as His representations of His own nature, to His revelation of the great system of grace under which He governs the world, and to His Word of revelation generally whether in whole or in part."[6]

When we speak of the integrity of God, then, we speak of more than just God's disposition toward an attribute we call honesty. His integrity is infinite. It not only touches His nature, but it floods His Word, the Bible. And His integrity is seen in all His attributes, just as all His attributes are seen in His integrity. He is honest in His holiness and holy in His honesty. He is honest in His justice and just in His honesty. He is infinitely honest and honest in His infinity.

Describing God's integrity, the Bible says, "He is the Rock, His work is perfect; for all His ways are justice, a God of truth and without injustice; righteous and upright is He" (Deut. 32:4 NKJV). The psalmist adds, "For the LORD is good; His mercy is everlasting, and His truth endures to all generations" (Ps. 100:5 NKJV).

The Honor of God

Charles Spurgeon once told of a poor, elderly woman who deeply loved the Lord, but was often the subject of ridicule by an unbelieving neighbor. Any talk of God brought instant criticism.

"How do you know that?" the neighbor would ask. The lady quickly would answer, "God tells me so a hundred times," and then she would quote verse after verse, usually from her favorite book of the Bible, John's first epistle. It is here that the phrase "we know" is used fourteen times.

One day the neighbor responded in skepticism, "But suppose God doesn't keep His Word?"

With a smile of confidence the saint replied, "His loss would be greater than mine. I would lose my soul. He would lose His honor."

The integrity of God is, indeed, a divine absolute as certain as are all of the characteristics of God combined. Not a praise word on our list fails the test of God's integrity. God is imminently, immutably and infinitely true. His justice is true; His mercy is true. His love is true; His kindness is true. His holiness is true and His faithfulness is true. What more can we say? God is truly, absolutely true! And that, beloved, is the truth.

Sunday

Father God . . . You are—TRUTHFUL!

TRUTH: The conformity to knowledge, fact, actuality or logic. The body of real things or facts. Fidelity to an established standard; exactness and genuineness.

Lord, You are the God of matchless integrity and infinite fidelity. I praise Your exacting and genuine character. Because of Your absolute integrity, I can trust the veracity of Your every word!
Your Word declares . . .

But you, O Lord, are a merciful and gracious God, slow to get angry, full of unfailing love and truth. Look down and have mercy on me. Give strength to your servant; yes, save me, for I am your servant.

Psalm 86:15–16

Give ear, O heavens, and I will speak; and hear, O earth, the words of my mouth. . . . For I proclaim the name of the LORD: Ascribe greatness to our God. He is the Rock, His work is perfect; for all His ways are justice, a God of truth and without injustice; righteous and upright is He.

Deuteronomy 32:1, 3–4 NKJV

Send out your light and your truth; let them guide me. Let them lead me to your holy mountain, to the place where you live. There I will go to the altar of God, to God—the source of all my joy. I will praise you with my harp, O God, my God!

Psalm 43:3–4

Lord . . . I Praise Your TRUTHFULNESS!

Monday

Father God . . . You are—KNOWING!

KNOWING: Having or reflecting knowledge, intelligence or information. The process of possessing direct cognition, awareness or understanding of truth. To be shrewdly and keenly alert.

Lord, I glory in the totality of Your absolute knowledge. You are altogether knowing in all that can possibly be known. Your awareness and understanding is limitless and Your intelligence and alertness are all-encompassing. Your Word declares . . .

Oh, what a wonderful God we have! How great are his riches and wisdom and knowledge! How impossible it is for us to understand his decisions and his methods! For who can know what the Lord is thinking? Who knows enough to be his counselor? . . . For everything comes from him; everything exists by his power and is intended for his glory. To him be glory evermore. Amen.

Romans 11:33–34, 36

It is by our actions that we know we are living in the truth, so we will be confident when we stand before the Lord, even if our hearts condemn us. For God is greater than our hearts, and he knows everything.

1 John 3:19–20

But God's truth stands firm like a foundation stone with this inscription: "The Lord knows those who are his," and

"Those who claim they belong to the Lord must turn away from all wickedness."

2 Timothy 2:19

If we had turned away from worshiping our God or spread our hands in prayer to foreign gods, God would surely have known it, for he knows the secrets of every heart.

Psalm 44:20–21

The Lord is good. When trouble comes, he is a strong refuge. And he knows everyone who trusts in him.

Nahum 1:7

Lord . . . I Praise Your KNOWLEDGE!

Tuesday

Father God . . . You are—PATIENT!

PATIENT: The bearing of pain or the facing of trials without complaint; to show self-control; to be serene, steady, unwavering and tolerant.

Lord, You are the fountainhead of all patience and tolerance. I rejoice that You came to earth in Your Son, Jesus Christ, to face the trials of human experience and suffer the pain of crucifixion that I might have eternal life. I glory in Your never-ending patience.
Your Word declares . . .

Such things were written in the Scriptures long ago to teach us. They give us hope and encouragement as we wait patiently for God's promises.
May God, who gives this patience and encouragement, help you live in complete harmony with each other—each with the attitude of Christ Jesus toward the other. Then all of you can join together with one voice, giving praise and glory to God, the Father of our Lord Jesus Christ.

Romans 15:4–6

Protect me, for I am devoted to you. Save me, for I serve you and trust you. You are my God. Be merciful, O Lord, for I am calling on you constantly. Give me happiness, O Lord, for my life depends on you. O Lord, you are so good, so ready to forgive, so full of unfailing love for all who ask your aid.

Psalm 86:2–5

And now, I pray, let the power of my Lord be great, just as You have spoken, saying, "The LORD is longsuffering and abundant in mercy, forgiving iniquity and transgression; but He by no means clears the guilty, visiting the iniquity of the fathers on the children to the third and fourth generation." Pardon the iniquity of this people, I pray, according to the greatness of Your mercy, just as You have forgiven this people, from Egypt even until now.

Numbers 14:17–19 NKJV

O God, the proud have risen against me. . . . But You, O Lord, are a God full of compassion, and gracious, longsuffering and abundant in mercy and truth.

Psalm 86:14–15 NKJV

Lord . . . I Praise Your PATIENCE!

Wednesday

Father God . . . You are—COMPLETE!

COMPLETE: That which exists in a state of entirety or wholeness. Lacking nothing necessary to make something whole. To be fully realized and entirely perfect. Absolute in makeup.

Lord, there is nothing that can be added to Your essence that might make You greater than You are, for You are fully and absolutely complete. All that You might possibly be, You already are, and that to infinity. I praise the entirety of Your essence.

Your Word declares . . .

For in Christ the fullness of God lives in a human body, and you are complete through your union with Christ. He is the Lord over every ruler and authority in the universe.

Colossians 2:9–10

He existed before everything else began, and he holds all creation together.

Christ is the head of the church, which is his body. He is the first of all who will rise from the dead, so he is first in everything. For God in all his fullness was pleased to live in Christ, and by him God reconciled everything to himself. He made peace with everything in heaven and on earth by means of his blood on the cross.

Colossians 1:17–20

I keep asking that the God of our Lord Jesus Christ, the glorious Father, may give you the Spirit of wisdom and revelation, so that you may know him better. . . . far above all rule and authority, power and dominion, and every title that can be given, not only in the present age but also in the one to come. And God placed all things under his feet and appointed him to be head over everything for the church, which is his body, the fullness of him who fills everything in every way.

Ephesians 1:17, 21–23 NIV

Oh, what a wonderful God we have! How great are his riches and wisdom and knowledge! How impossible it is for us to understand his decisions and his methods! For who can know what the Lord is thinking? Who knows enough to be his counselor? And who could ever give him so much that he would have to pay it back? For everything comes from him; everything exists by his power and is intended for his glory. To him be glory evermore. Amen.

Romans 11:33–36

The highest heavens and the earth and everything in it all belong to the Lord your God.

Deuteronomy 10:14

Lord . . . I Praise Your COMPLETENESS!

Thursday

Father God . . . You are—GRACIOUS!

GRACIOUS: That which is marked by a spirit of kindness and courtesy. To be amiable, genial and loving. Of or pertaining to the rendering of grace as an unmerited gift.

Lord, You are wondrously and unspeakably kind. I rejoice in Your amiable, genial nature. Your dealings with men are marked by a spirit of caring concern. I glory in Your unmerited favor.

Your Word declares . . .

Yet the LORD longs to be gracious to you; he rises to show you compassion. For the LORD is a God of justice. Blessed are all who wait for him!

O people of Zion, who live in Jerusalem, you will weep no more. How gracious he will be when you cry for help! As soon as he hears, he will answer you.

Isaiah 30:18–19 NIV

The LORD is gracious and righteous; our God is full of compassion. The LORD protects the simplehearted; when I was in great need, he saved me.

Psalm 116:5–6 NIV

179

That is why the Lord says, "Turn to me now, while there is time! Give me your hearts. Come with fasting, weeping, and mourning. Don't tear your clothing in your grief; instead, tear your hearts." Return to the Lord your God, for he is gracious and merciful. He is not easily angered. He is filled with kindness and is eager not to punish you.

Joel 2:12–13

Lord . . . I Praise Your GRACE!

Friday

Father God . . . You are—VICTORIOUS!

VICTORIOUS: Characteristic of or expressing a sense of overcoming an enemy or antagonist. The achievement of mastery or success in a struggle against an opponent or obstacle. The quality of being triumphant in a campaign.

Lord, with delight I praise the victory of Your mighty essence. You are the God of everlasting triumph. Joyfully I acknowledge the mastery of Your never-failing name! Your Word declares . . .

How we thank God, who gives us victory over sin and death through Jesus Christ our Lord!

So, my dear brothers and sisters, be strong and steady, always enthusiastic about the Lord's work, for you know that nothing you do for the Lord is ever useless.

1 Corinthians 15:57–58

All your sons will be taught by the LORD, and great will be your children's peace. . . . If anyone does attack you, it will not be my doing; whoever attacks you will surrender to you. . . . no weapon forged against you will prevail, and you will refute every tongue that accuses you. This is the heritage of the servants of the LORD, and this is their vindication from me.

Isaiah 54:13, 15, 17 NIV

Give us aid against the enemy, for the help of man is worthless. With God we will gain the victory, and he will trample down our enemies.

Psalm 60:11–12 NIV

When you go out to fight your enemies and you face horses and chariots and an army greater than your own, do not be afraid. The LORD your God, who brought you safely out of Egypt, is with you! . . . For the LORD your God is going with you! He will fight for you against your enemies, and he will give you victory!

Deuteronomy 20:1, 4

I chased my enemies and caught them; I did not stop until they were conquered. I struck them down so they could not get up; they fell beneath my feet. You have armed me with strength for the battle; you have subdued my enemies under my feet.

Psalm 18:37–39

Can anything ever separate us from Christ's love? Does it mean he no longer loves us if we have trouble or calamity, or are persecuted, or are hungry or cold or in danger or threatened with death? (Even the Scriptures say, "For your sake we are killed every day; we are being slaughtered like sheep.") No, despite all these things, overwhelming victory is ours through Christ, who loved us.

Romans 8:35–37

Lord . . . I Praise Your VICTORY!

Saturday

Father God . . . You are—GOOD!

GOOD: Of or possessing a favorable character or nature. That which is comely, agreeable, pleasant and whole. To be honorable, ethical and satisfying.

Lord, all that our word *good* describes has its roots in Your essence. Your character is altogether wholesome and Your nature abundantly satisfying. Your every act is honorable and Your myriad dealings are pleasant. You are marvelously and infinitely good!

Your Word declares . . .

Taste and see that the LORD is good. Oh, the joys of those who trust in him! Let the LORD's people show him reverence, for those who honor him will have all they need.

Psalm 34:8–9

Acknowledge that the LORD is God! . . . Enter his gates with thanksgiving; go into his courts with praise. Give thanks to him and bless his name. For the LORD is good. His unfailing love continues forever, and his faithfulness continues to each generation.

Psalm 100:3–5

The Lord is good and does what is right; he shows the proper path to those who go astray. He leads the humble in what is right, teaching them his way.

Psalm 25:8–9

The Lord is wonderfully good to those who wait for him and seek him. So it is good to wait quietly for salvation from the Lord.

Lamentations 3:25–26

Related references—Nahum 1:7; Psalm 135:3.
Lord . . . I Praise Your GOODNESS!

Summary for Week Seven

Father God, You Are . . .
    TRUTHFUL,
        KNOWING,
            PATIENT
                and COMPLETE;
    GRACIOUS,
        VICTORIOUS
            and GOOD!

The Praise Page

This seven-week focus also may be used as a seven-day focus (see the "day" designation in parentheses for each cluster). This would enable you to "stand amazed" in praise daily and saturate each week in the nature and character of God.

Week One:

Father God, You Are . . .
  LOVING, TIMELESS, PRESENT and UNIQUE;
  SPOTLESS, GLORIOUS and GREAT!
(Monday)

Week Two:

Father God, You Are . . .
  HOLY, EXCELLENT, RELIABLE and STRONG;
  SUFFICIENT, MEASURELESS and WISE!
(Tuesday)

Week Three:

Father God, You Are . . .
  MAJESTIC, CREATIVE, AVAILABLE and MIGHTY;
  STEADFAST, GENEROUS and ABLE!
(Wednesday)

Week Four:

Father God, You Are . . .
   JUST, INVINCIBLE, BEAUTIFUL and KIND;
      RESPONSIVE, CHANGELESS and FORGIVING!
(Thursday)

Week Five:

Father God, You Are . . .
   FAITHFUL, POWERFUL, HEALTHFUL and SECURE;
      PEACEFUL, RADIANT and RIGHTEOUS!
(Friday)

Week Six:

Father God, You Are . . .
   MERCIFUL, JOYFUL, INFINITE and STABLE;
      WONDERFUL, ACCESSIBLE
         and SOVEREIGN!
(Saturday)

Week Seven:

Father God, You Are . . .
   TRUTHFUL, KNOWING, PATIENT and COMPLETE;
      GRACIOUS, VICTORIOUS and GOOD!
(Sunday)

To further enrich your understanding of praise, I recommend the use of good sacred "worship" music in your personal time of prayer. I have been especially blessed by the unique worship CDs of Terry MacAlmon, recorded live at the World Prayer Center in Colorado Springs, Colorado. For information on these CDs, contact:

Terry MacAlmon Ministries
P.O. Box 62501
Colorado Springs, CO 80962

You may also wish to read my trilogy on delighting in the Lord through intercessory worship, which includes *Heights of Delight, Pathways of Delight* and *Rivers of Delight* (published by Regal Books, Ventura, California).

Notes

Part 1: *The Object of Our Praise*

1. A. W. Tozer, *The Knowledge of the Holy* (New York: Harper & Row, 1975), 34.
2. William Burt Pope, *A Compendium of Christian Theology,* vol. 1 (New York: Hunt & Eaton, 1890), 289.
3. Ibid., 353.
4. Julian of Norwich, *Revelations of Divine Love,* 7th ed. (London: Methune & Co., Ltd., 1920), 14–15.
5. Herman Bavinck, *The Doctrine of God* (Grand Rapids: Baker, 1977), 139.
6. James I. Packer, *Knowing God* (Downers Grove, Ill.: InterVarsity Press, 1973), 15.
7. Ibid., 17.
8. Ibid., 18.
9. Ibid.
10. Ibid., 21–22.
11. Ibid., 30.
12. Ibid., 29.
13. Ibid., 24.
14. Bavinck, *The Doctrine of God,* 127.
15. Ibid., 120–21.
16. Pope, *A Compendium of Christian Theology,* 287.
17. Bavinck, *The Doctrine of God,* 126.
18. Ibid., 131.
19. Ibid., 121.
20. Pope, *A Compendium of Christian Theology,* 289.
21. Packer, *Knowing God,* 30.
22. Tozer, *The Knowledge of the Holy,* 20–21.
23. Bavinck, *The Doctrine of God,* 129–30.
24. Pope, *A Compendium of Christian Theology,* 287.
25. Bavinck, *The Doctrine of God,* 134.
26. Tozer, *The Knowledge of the Holy,* 21.
27. Pope, *A Compendium of Christian Theology,* 287.
28. Bavinck, *The Doctrine of God,* 117.
29. Ibid, 124–25.
30. Ibid., 125.
31. Pope, *A Compendium of Christian Theology,* 293.
32. Ibid., 295.
33. Ibid., 296–97.
34. Ibid., 300.
35. Ibid., 301.
36. Ibid., 303.
37. Ibid., 356.
38. Ibid., 357.
39. Packer, *Knowing God,* 16.
40. Ibid., 13–14.
41. Brother Lawrence, *The Practice of the Presence of God* (Old Tappan, N.J.: Revell, 1959), 25.

Part 2: *The Content of Our Praise*

Week One

1. John Bisagno, *God Is* (Wheaton: Victor, 1983), 20.
2. Ibid., 18.
3. Ibid., 19.
4. James I. Packer, *Knowing God* (Downers Grove, Ill.: InterVarsity Press, 1973), 35.
5. A. W. Tozer, *The Knowledge of the Holy* (New York: Harper & Row, 1975), 106.
6. Ibid., 105.
7. Packer, *Knowing God*, 114.
8. Bisagno, *God Is*, 20–21.
9. Tozer, *The Knowledge of the Holy*, 109.
10. Ibid., 107.
11. Packer, *Knowing God*, 37.
12. Tozer, *The Knowledge of the Holy*, 107.
13. St. Anselm, *Proslogium* (La Salle, Ill.: Open Court Publishing Co., 1903), 6.

Week Two

1. Arthur W. Pink, *The Attributes of God* (Grand Rapids: Baker, 1975), 41.
2. Ibid.
3. John Bisagno, *God Is* (Wheaton: Victor, 1983), 44.
4. A. W. Tozer, *The Knowledge of the Holy* (New York: Harper & Row, 1975), 112–13.
5. Pink, *The Attributes of God*, 42.
6. William Burt Pope, *A Compendium of Christian Theology*, vol. 1 (New York: Hunt & Eaton, 1890), 333–34.
7. Tozer, *The Knowledge of the Holy*, 113.
8. Herman Bavinck, *The Doctrine of God* (Grand Rapids: Baker, 1977), 209–10.
9. Ibid., 210–11.
10. Bisagno, *God Is*, 45–46.
11. Bavinck, *The Doctrine of God*, 213.
12. Ibid., 214.
13. Tozer, *The Knowledge of the Holy*, 113.
14. Pink, *The Attributes of God*, 43.
15. Bisagno, *God Is*, 49.
16. Bavinck, *The Doctrine of God*, 212.
17. Ibid., 213.
18. Bisagno, *God Is*, 51.
19. Pope, *A Compendium of Christian Theology*, 333.
20. Ibid.
21. Ibid., 331.
22. Pink, *The Attributes of God*, 41.
23. Tozer, *The Knowledge of the Holy*, 112.
24. Bisagno, *God Is*, 43.
25. Tozer, *The Knowledge of the Holy*, 111.
26. Pope, *A Compendium of Christian Theology*, 304.
27. Pink, *The Attributes of God*, 42.
28. Ibid.

Week Three

1. James I. Packer, *Knowing God* (Downers Grove, Ill.: InterVarsity Press, 1973), 73.
2. Ibid.
3. Herman Bavinck, *The Doctrine of God* (Grand Rapids: Baker, 1977), 127.
4. Ibid., 115–16.
5. Arthur W. Pink, *The Attributes of God* (Grand Rapids: Baker, 1975), 30.
6. Bavinck, *The Doctrine of God*, 140.
7. Packer, *Knowing God*, 78.
8. A. W. Tozer, *The Knowledge of the Holy* (New York: Harper & Row, 1975), 40.

9. "Beginnings: The First Moments," *National Geographic*, June 1983, 738–44.

10. Ibid., 744.

Week Four

1. William Burt Pope, *A Compendium of Christian Theology*, vol. 1 (New York: Harper & Row, 1975), 335.

2. A. W. Tozer, *The Knowledge of the Holy* (New York: Harper & Row, 1975), 93.

3. Ibid.

4. Herman Bavinck, *The Doctrine of God* (Grand Rapids: Baker, 1977), 217–18.

5. John Bisagno, *God Is* (Wheaton: Victor, 1983), 65.

6. Ibid., 66.

7. Ibid., 67.

8. Ibid., 71.

9. Ibid., 68.

10. Bavinck, *The Doctrine of God*, 217–18.

11. Bisagno, *God Is*, 66.

12. Tozer, *The Knowledge of the Holy*, 94.

13. Pope, *A Compendium of Christian Theology*, 336.

14. Ibid.

Week Five

1. Arthur W. Pink, *The Attributes of God* (Grand Rapids: Baker, 1975), 52.

2. Ibid.

3. William Burt Pope, *A Compendium of Christian Theology*, vol. 1 (New York: Hunt & Eaton, 1890), 343–44.

4. John Bisagno, *God Is* (Wheaton: Victor, 1983), 110.

Week Six

1. John Bisagno, *God Is* (Wheaton: Victor, 1983), 53–54.

2. Arthur W. Pink, *The Attributes of God* (Grand Rapids: Baker, 1975), 72.

3. William Burt Pope, *A Compendium of Christian Theology*, vol. 1 (New York: Hunt & Eaton, 1890), 346–47.

4. Bisagno, *God Is*, 55.

5. Ibid., 56.

6. A. W. Tozer, *The Knowledge of the Holy* (New York: Harper & Row, 1975), 96.

7. Pink, *The Attributes of God*, 72.

8. Ibid., 76.

9. Bisagno, *God Is*, 56.

10. Tozer, *The Knowledge of the Holy*, 96–97.

11. Ibid., 97.

12. Ibid.

13. Pink, *The Attributes of God*, 74–75.

14. Tozer, *The Knowledge of the Holy*, 96.

Week Seven

1. William Burt Pope, *A Compendium of Christian Theology*, vol. 1 (New York: Hunt & Eaton, 1890), 342.

2. Herman Bavinck, *The Doctrine of God* (Grand Rapids: Baker, 1977), 201.

3. Pope, *A Compendium of Christian Theology*, 342.

4. Bavinck, *The Doctrine of God*, 202.

5. Ibid., 201–2

6. Pope, *A Compendium of Christian Theology*, 342.

Dick Eastman is president of Every Home for Christ and originator of Change the World School of Prayer. He has also written *The Hour That Changes the World* and *No Easy Read*.

THE HOUR THAT
CHANGES THE WORLD
*A Practical Plan
for Personal Prayer
25th anniversary edition*

A Classic Book with a 21st Century Challenge

More than two million Christians around the world have revitalized their prayer lives through the step-by-step plan of prayer outlined in this book. You'll be challenged to spend one hour each day in prayer by dividing the hour into twelve five-minute "points of focus," such as praise, waiting, confession and Scripture praying, which will help you to develop a more consistent habit of daily prayer.

This special 25th anniversary edition features a new introduction by Dick Eastman and a new foreword by Joni Eareckson Tada, in which she writes: *"The Hour That Changes the World* may appear small and modest, but don't let its size fool you. Full of biblical insights about prayer, packed with testimonies of prayer warriors from years past, brimming with practical suggestions that will help you carve out a purposeful time of praise and intercession, Dick Eastman's book is arguably the most significant book on prayer written in modern times."